Birman Cats

The moral rights of the author has been asserted
British Library Cataloguing in Publication Data
A catalogue record for this book is available from the British Library

ISBN 978-1-909820-49-4

Disclaimer and Legal Notice

Birman Cats

**The Complete Owners Guide to
Birman Cats and Kittens**
*Including Buying, Daily Care, Personality,
Temperament, Health,
Diet and Breeders*

Colette Anderson

Foreword

The first Birman cat I ever saw was sitting on top of a refrigerator. I was in graduate school at the time, and helping one of my dearest friends Julie move into a new apartment.

I walked into the "old" kitchen to start packing dishes, glanced up, and was stopped in my tracks by the bluest eyes I'd ever seen on any creature, feline or human.

The cat let out a soft little "mew," I put my hand up to scratch her ears, and Pumpkin and I were friends for life. That's actually about all it takes with a Birman thanks to their lovely, people-oriented dispositions.

Pumpkin's native curiosity soon compelled her down from her perch, and when Julie came in the kitchen, I was receiving a great deal of "help" wrapping glassware in newspaper.

Over the next three years while we finished our master's degrees, Pumpkin provided even more of her particularly insightful guidance on everything from research papers to final exams.

Julie and I were assigned to grade tests for the same professor, and nothing delighted Pumpkin more than the long evenings we spent sitting on the floor surrounded by blue exam books and an inviting litter of red pens.

I have no idea how many of those pens wound up under the furniture courtesy of her white-gloved paws, but we always seemed to be running to the office supply place for more.

Pumpkin helped us write and proofread our respective theses, and Julie, in a waggish bit of feline devotion, included the cleverly misspelled name P.C. Berman in her acknowledgements for "Pumpkin Cat Birman."

Eleven years after we received our degrees, I got a call from Julie telling me of Pumpkin's passing at the venerable age of 16 years. I was genuinely saddened by the news, and still think of that gorgeous cat with real affection.

I have known many Birmans since, but Pumpkin was the first, and an absolute banner representative of her breed in every way. These hardy, healthy cats are not just physically beautifully; they're also incredibly personable. A Birman in the house is, simply put, a presence like no other.

There are certainly things to consider before you adopt a semi-longhaired cat like a Birman. These are social cats, and although they are adaptable to your schedule, they don't like to be left alone for long periods of time.

For this reason, Birmans are not necessarily well suited to be "only children," and often thrive best with people who work from home or who have other pets.

They do require a grooming commitment, and are a long-lived breed, surviving 12-16 years. In exchange, you are afforded the opportunity to share your life with a highly intelligent, soft-voiced cat whose companionship will be constant and loving. Among the oriental breeds, the Birman is definitely my favorite.

In the following pages, I will introduce you to the Birman, and explain its needs in terms of daily and veterinary care. If you have never owned a cat before, the Birman is an excellent breed with which to begin if you are willing to put in the time to keep its coat in good shape.

The great news on that front is that a Birman's coat doesn't tangle like other longhaired cats because these animals have no undercoat. That allows you to enjoy the plushness of their silky fur without the potential headache of dealing with mats.

Birmans are definitely not outdoor cats – as I will explain, no cats belong outdoors in my opinion – but Birmans in particular are house pets. Beyond the need to keep their coats in good shape, their dispositions are too peaceful and trusting to be turned loose in a world filled with dangers.

If, however, you are looking for a beautiful, devoted, healthy, and long-lived feline companion to share your home, you may well have found the perfect match in the blue-eyed, white-gloved Birman.

Acknowledgments

I would like to thank and dedicate this book to my dear friend Julie and in memory of all those wonderful years in college together. The joy and fun we had is so vividly etched in my mind with so many experiences good and bad being shared with Pumpkin who was always there when we needed her most.

To my wonderful husband Nick, thank you again for all your help and assistance and for undertaking the dreaded proof reading. His observations and comments are as always invaluable and without his encouragement I don't think I'd have ever started this enjoyable journey.

Just a note to say that I have written this book using American spelling as that is what I'm used to. I have given measurements in both feet and inches/pounds and ounces and also in metric. I have also given costs in US$ and GBP. Both the measurements and costs are approximate guides. I have done my best to ensure the accuracy of the information in this book as at the time of publication.

Table of Contents

Chapter 1 – Introduction

K nown as the "Sacred Cat of Burma," Birmans are exceptionally striking cats with their silky coats and incredible blue eyes. They pad through our lives on pure white feet; markings that, according to legend, were earned by the great loyalty and affection these cats show for their humans.

History of the Birman Breed

According to the most accepted origin myth, the beautiful coloration of the Birman breed was the result of an act of loyalty on the part of a cat that was the companion of a priest in the Temple of Lao-Tsun in Northern Burma on Mount Lugh.

When raiders fatally wounded the priest, the faithful cat placed his paws on the body of his dying master. As the cat gazed at a statue of the goddess Tsun-Kyan-Kse, the animal's fur took on a golden hue and his yellow eyes turned as blue as glittering sapphires.

The cat's legs turned brown, but where the paws rested on the head of the priest, the feet remained pure white. By morning, all of the cats in the temple had the same golden fur and white feet.

The priest's cat still had more work to do in service of his master, however. Seven days later, the animal died in order to carry the priest's soul to paradise. Now, when one of the sacred cats of the Temple of Lao-Tsun passes, it is believed that the soul of a priest goes with it into the afterlife.

Departing from legend and back into recorded history, the temple, located in northern Burma, was left unmolested until early in the 20th century.

Two westerners, August Pavie and Major Gordon Russell supposedly helped the priests during some upset during this period and were rewarded with a pair of the sacred cats in 1919 as a gesture of gratitude.

The Birman cats were sent to the men in France, but the male died in passage. The female was pregnant and successfully delivered a litter of kittens in her new home. The Cat Club de France recognized Birmans in France as a distinct breed in 1925.

During World War II, the breed was reduced to a single pair named Orloff and Xenia de Kaabaa. Their kittens (Manou, Lon saito, Sjaipour, Sita 1 and Sita 2) formed the foundation for the breed's comeback after the war.

It was necessary to outcross to other longhaired breeds including Persians and Siamese, but the result was that pure Birmans were once again being produced by the early 1950s.

In the early 1960s, a fancier, Mrs. Elsie Fisher of the Praha cattery, brought some of these Birmans to the UK. The breed was introduced in the United States at roughly the same time.

The Governing Council of the Cat Fancy in the UK recognized Birmans as a distinct breed in 1966, with the U.S. Cat Fancier's Association following suit in 1967. Birmans gained recognition from the Canadian Cat Association and The International Cat Association in 1979.

Physical Characteristics

The Birman is a medium to large cat with a strong build. Males are slightly larger than females, with the breed overall averaging 8 - 12 lbs. / 3.63 - 5.44 kg. They have striking blue eyes that are round and quite large set above a distinctly Roman nose.

Their expression is open and sweet, at an almost amusing variance with their walk, which is tiger-like and predatory. Birmans should have broad faces and their ears are ideally as wide at the base as they are tall. The lifespan for the breed is 12-16 years.

Confusion with Other Breeds

Birmans are often confused with six other types of cat. These include:

- The Siamese, which is a shorthaired cat with color points. Siamese cats are long and slender and their heads form a pronounced wedge.

- The Burmese, which is also a shorthaired cat. This breed is solid colored, without pointing and has gold eyes.

- The Balinese, which has a body much like that of the Siamese, but with long, silky fur.

- The Himalayan, a longhaired cat with color points, but a thick cobby body and flat face like its Persian relatives.

- The Ragdoll, a color-pointed cat with long hair, but many varying patterns of white. (Birmans were used in the development of this breed.)

- The Snowshoe, a color-pointed cat with short hair and many varying patterns of white.

Coat, Markings, and Colorations

Birmans have medium length silky hair that does not mat like that of similar breeds because these cats do not have an undercoat. Even with their plush coats, they shed very little.

Their feet are always pure white, which sets them apart from all the other breeds with which they are commonly confused.

Birman kittens are born all white, with the points coming in after about a week for the darker colors and two weeks for the lighter or "clear" points. The coat develops slowly and does not reach its full quality and length for two years.

Gloves and Laces

The white marking on a Birman's feet is called the "glove." It should go across the front feet in a very even line and be perfectly symmetrical on each foot.

In the back, the glove also covers the foot, but it extends up the back of the hock and ends in a distinct point. This marking is known as the laces or gauntlets.

A Birman's gloving is the critical decision in whether an individual is show or pet quality. Too much or too little white on the feet can make all the difference to the critical eye.

Accepted Points

The first Birmans were bred as seal points, with blue points introduced in 1959 through breeding programs incorporating blue Persians.

All point colors are acceptable for the breed, but seal and blue are most common. Other point types include chocolate, red, lilac, and cream. Tabby and tortie points are seen in seal, lilac, blue, and chocolate.

Templecat Shorthair Birman

Since 2008, Birman breeders in New Zealand, have worked to develop a shorthair version of the breed they call the Templecat Shorthair Birman.

The short coat was initially achieved by mating a Birman with a cinnamon spotted Oriental. The breeding program has now achieved shorthaired versions in seal, blue, chocolate, lilac, cinnamon, and fawn by using full registered Birmans.

These cats are as warm-natured and friendly as their longhaired cousins, with docile dispositions. Their coats have a slightly springy feel, but are silky to the touch and easily maintained.

Sometimes simply referred to as the Templecat, these shorthaired Birmans are still quite rare and the breed is considered to still be in its developmental stages.

The Personality of the Birman

The Birman is a genuinely sweet cat with a superb disposition. They have a reputation for being incredibly easy to handle. Their quick intelligence makes them fast learners and among the most adaptable of all breeds.

They are perfectly agreeable to tailoring their daily schedule to your comings and goings, and are quiet cats with small voices. Your Birman will get lonely, however, if you're away from home a lot, and will definitely be waiting at the door when you come back.

Every Birman I've ever known has an almost uncanny ability to recognize and associate the slightest sounds. Don't expect to sneak into the house or pretend to be asleep when these cats want breakfast first thing in the day.

While you're home, you'll have a curious and social companion by your side. This is definitely a "people" breed. While a Birman's fondness for being a lap cat varies by individual, you can count on these cats to be with you and interested in whatever you're doing.

Overall, this is an active and playful companion breed with a gentle way of interacting and a quiet, unobtrusive manner when they're simply spending time with their people.

Male or Female?

The "male or female" question is fairly standard, but with most breeds, including the Birman, I've found that it really doesn't matter all that much. Both are equally personable and easy going. I've seen little difference in personality based on gender.

In general, I'm much more prone to take cats on an individual basis and to consider the factor of environment in the development of temperament. Many Birman breeders, however, say they find the females to be a little less likely to cuddle, whereas neutered male Birmans have a reputation for being complete attention hogs.

For the most part, I've always had male cats irrespective of breed because they tend to be larger and I like big cats. I do agree with the statement that neutered males turn into lovable lugs as soon as the excess testosterone is out of their system.

Some people shy away from owning male cats due to the potential for urine spraying, but I don't see this as a problem. I have never had a tom that sprayed in the house. The behavior is extremely rare with neutered males and has been, in my opinion, blown out of proportion.

More than One?

Even though Birmans don't suffer from the kind of loud and mournful separation anxiety seen in breeds like the Siamese, they will get lonely. If you spend long periods of time out of the house, or worse yet, out of town, you will definitely want more than one cat.

I am personally a big advocate of adopting littermates. Obviously with a pedigreed breed like the Birman, this can be expensive, but the long-term benefits are considerable. The special bond that siblings enjoy seems to keep the animals more kittenish and playful as they age.

I've lived with two Russian Blue males, brothers, for a number of years and they wrestle just as vigorously at ten years of age as they did when they were gawky adolescents. They're wonderful company for one another when I'm away and definitely double trouble when it comes to thinking up creative things to get into.

Although Birmans have a propensity to be the alpha cat with other breeds, they get on with a proper egalitarian air with one another.

With other Pets

Although adaptable as a breed, Birmans do get lonely for their humans if you are gone from the home for a long period of time. For this reason, they get on quite well with other animals, including dogs.

Ideally, you will be able to have two cats at one time. Bear in mind, however, that Birmans have very "alpha" dispositions. If you have one Birman and a cat of any other breed, the Birman will be the boss and will expect to be the center of all attention and affection.

This doesn't translate as aggression, however. It's almost as if the Birman presents the other cat with a memo stating, "I'm in charge. You're good with that. Done deal."

With Children

Birmans do extremely well with children even though these cats do not like to be picked up or to be held tightly. If a Birman doesn't like how the interaction with children is progressing, he simply walks away rather than displaying aggression toward the child.

Unlike many breeds, the Birman is very patient. Like all cats, they can "disappear" completely when they don't approve of things, reappearing as if by magic when circumstances are more to their liking.

Do not, however, rely completely on the cat's patience to govern its relationship with a child. Teach children to interact gently and kindly with animals of all types.

Any pet experiencing pain or fear is capable of responding in an adverse fashion regardless of how gentle the animal may be. While certainly you do not want your child to be endangered, I often ask parents to think about who is really at fault in the exchange.

Explain to your child that Birmans don't like to be picked up because they're big cats who feel better when they have all four feet on the ground.

Often children just want the animal to stay near them, which the Birman is quite happy to do as long as he's not being carted around or physically restrained. If your child understands these things, their relationship with the cat should be quite good.

Inside or Out?

Obviously a pedigreed cat like a Birman is an expensive investment. Also, longhaired cats do not make good outside cats because exposure to the elements and vegetation greatly complicates caring for their coats.

Beyond those considerations, however, I do not believe any cat, including the very hardy Domestic Shorthair, often referred to as an "alley cat," should be allowed outside.

My cats have been exclusively indoor pets for the more than 40 years that I have had feline companions. I do not believe they have suffered any deprivation, and, in fact, have benefited enormously. Many of my pets have lived well in excess of 15 years regardless of breed.

Our modern world is a dangerous place for our beloved animal companions. Whether that danger arises from automobiles, aggressive dogs, wildlife, or bad humans, the risk is not worth it in my opinion. I would never dream of allowing my cats access to the outside world.

There are many cat owners who achieve a compromise position by designing some kind of secure enclosed structure that allows their cats to be contained while enjoying sunlight and fresh air and the sounds of the outside world.

I have done this with my pets, and so long as you can securely bring your cat in and out of the structure, I think this is an excellent idea. There are no set designs for these kinds of enclosures, but you can easily find many good ideas online through your favorite search engine.

Pros and Cons

Assembling a set of "pros" and "cons" associated with any type of animal is not as simple as some people think. These things are very much a matter of personal perception.

I was raised around dogs and am very fond of them, but I have no desire to keep a dog as a pet because I don't want to have to walk one. Other people think the walks are absolutely the best part of dog ownership.

In terms of their affectionate and docile personalities, Birmans are fantastic cats. They do exhibit some minor separation anxiety that manifests mainly as loneliness, so I really don't recommend them as "only children" for busy, on-the-good owners.

While your Birman won't be underfoot, he will be close by and very interested in whatever you're doing. Since I'm someone who actively talks to my cats, I love this trait of the breed. If you want a more ornamental cat that will position itself attractively on the sofa and look on aloofly, you might do better with a Persian.

Frankly, the biggest argument against having any longhaired cat is the need for a consistent grooming schedule. Fortunately, this does not mean daily combing and brushing with a Birman.

Because the Birman has no undercoat, their silky fur is not bad to tangle, and mats are less of an issue. Certainly grooming is involved with this breed, but not to the intense degree seen with the Persian.

All in all, the Birman is an excellent companion animal. They are physically stunning animals with their classic beauty and regal posture, and truly lovely friends with sweet and mild dispositions.

Chapter 2 – Finding Your Birman Cat

People who have not gone through the process of purchasing a pedigree cat may have some completely erroneous assumptions about what will happen when they visit a cattery.

If you think that you are simply going to drop in, pick a kitten, and pay for it, you need to sit down. It's not going to be that simple, and you may get turned down. Yes. You may get turned down.

If a breeder doesn't think you're a good candidate to raise one of their kittens, they don't have to do business with you — and they won't.

Understanding Breeder Requirements

Expect to be required to sign a written contract that will have some or all of the following stipulations:

- Sometime in the 72 hours following the adoption, you will take the kitten to a qualified veterinarian for a complete health evaluation. You will need to provide proof that this visit has occurred.

- Your agreement that the cat you adopt will be spayed or neutered before it reaches 6 months of age and that you will provide proof of this fact in order to gain possession of the cat's papers.

In addition, you will be asked questions about your home life, your schedule, and your prior experience with cats and with the Birman breed.

If you need to, adjust your attitude now! The breeder is not being a jerk or being nosy. They're doing their job — putting the welfare of the cats they raise first.

You may be asked things like, "Where do you plan for the kitten to sleep?" or "What do you intend to feed your cat?" Be honest with your answers. Don't try to "game" a breeder. It generally backfires.

If this is your first time to have a cat as a pet or to have this breed, say so. Ask questions. For instance, you might say something like, "My last cat loved to sleep on the bed. What do Birmans usually prefer? I'll get the kitten whatever kind of bed he'd like best".

Breeders want to know that the kitten is going to a good home with loving and attentive "parents". Don't be at all surprised if the breeder calls you up during the first few weeks to check on the progress of the transition. You want this to happen!

Making friends with your breeder gives you access to someone who knows Birman cats well and can answer your questions. This is an important relationship, and one you want to cultivate.

Formulating Your Own Questions

Adopting a pedigree cat should be a process of give and take on both sides in the exchange of information. Any breeder who is not willing to answer your questions should be considered suspect.

In truth, talking to a breeder about their cattery usually opens the floodgates of information. Most are not only willing to talk about their cats, they're impossible to stop!

There are, however, some definite areas that you want to cover pre-adoption. Be sure that you go over these points to your satisfaction.

- Have the kitten's parents been healthy throughout their lives?

- Does the cattery maintain complete health records on all their cats and are you free to examine those records?

- Can you meet and interact with the kitten's parents?

- Has the kitten received any vaccinations and if so, when are the booster shots to be administered?

- Will you receive copies of all of the kitten's records at the time of adoption?

- Are there any specific health problems associated with Birman cats and has the kitten been evaluated for those issues?

- Has the kitten seen a vet for any other reason? If so, why and what treatment was administered?

- What is the nature of the health guarantee that is part of the adoption agreement?

- Has the kitten had fleas and has it required deworming?

- Ask for a complete summary of all veterinary care the kitten has received and copies of the complete records to pass on to your own veterinarian.

Understand that a kitten that has had or even does have fleas is not the end of the world. Catteries fight fleas on an ongoing basis. You just want to make sure that the "passengers" have disembarked from the baby before it comes into your home. Eradicating fleas can be a time consuming and exhausting process once they are established.

Also ask for the breeder's references. These should include people who have adopted kittens from the cattery in the past and who are willing to talk to you about the experience — both in terms of interaction with the breeder and their experience with the cat as a pet.

Ask About Socialization

In most cases catteries keep kittens until they are at least 3 months of age. This ensures that when the babies are adopted they have been fully weaned and they've become trained in the "basics," like litter box and scratching post use.

I'll discuss both of these things in greater detail later in the book, but you do want to specifically ask what kind of box and litter the kitten is accustomed to using and what kind of scratching surface.

The best way to reinforce and encourage good behavior in a newly adopted kitten is to keep everything exactly the same. For a smooth transition, use the same kind of box, litter, and post, only introducing changes gradually as the kitten grows.

Also find out how the breeder works with the kitten to make sure that it is well socialized. Some of the hallmarks of a good program of socialization include:

- Daily handling

- Free exploration time

- Interaction with other cats and kittens

- Intellectual stimulation (toys and games)

- Supervised exposure to dogs and/or children

- Comfort level with reasonable noise

Kittens that have gotten used to these kinds of environmental factors early on tend to show much less nervousness as adult cats and more flexibility and adaptability to changes in their immediate surroundings.

Birmans have a reputation for being social cats that love to spend time with their humans, but the importance of early socialization cannot be overstated. Cats are individuals and they will react to the manner in which they are raised.

If you've ever seen those funny cartoons that suggest pets and owners look alike, you may understand this point more fully. A nervous person tends to have nervous pets; a grumpy person's pets may be irascible, and so on.

Although Birman cats are docile by nature, if truly pushed to their limits, they will react. That being said, however, any cat will display ill temper if something is going on that frightens, threatens, or simply displeases it.

Most breeders are in agreement, however, that a well socialized cat of any breed will be much more likely to exhibit the most positive qualities of its kind.

Judging the Health of a Kitten

You are not just visiting a cattery to inspect the facilities and to be evaluated by the breeder, you are also there to look at cats — which is actually the best part!

Always ask permission to handle the cats. Even though it's assumed that you are there to do so, it's just polite. If you're asked to use a hand sanitizer first, don't be offended.

Many feline diseases are so easily transmissible they can be passed from one cat to another with just a nose tap. Sanitizing your hands is for the protection of the cats, and not a reflection on you.

When you are handling the kittens, pay attention to all the following factors:

- The kitten's coat should be soft, clean, and completely intact. There should be no evidence of thin spots or any missing patches of hair.

- Very gently blow on the fur to create a parting. Look at the skin. There should be no flaking, which would indicate that the skin is dry.

- Look behind the ears, in the "arm pits," and at the base of the tail. These are the prime locations for evidence of flea "dirt," small accumulations of what looks like tiny gravel, but is actually excreted blood from the fleas.

- Take a good look at the baby's eyes. You should be met with a bright, curious gaze that is both interested and sweet. The eyes should not be "runny" with discharge, and there should be no crusting in the corners.

- Also look inside the ears. The flaps should be pink and healthy in appearance and the ear canal should be clean and free of black, tarry debris. There should be no odor, especially one that smells of yeast.

- Also check the kitten's nostrils for any sign of discharge.

- The baby should not be sneezing or otherwise sniffling.

Don't be surprised if the kitten is a little shy when you're first introduced. That's normal. Within minutes, however, you should be interacting with a little ball of madcap energy!

Expect Paperwork

You are, after all, engaging in a transaction, so anticipate a fair amount of paperwork. The basic agreement will include the following:

- A description of the Birman breed.

- A description of the color and pattern of the specific individual being adopted.

- The gender of the kitten.

- The agreed upon price.

- The names of the parents.

- Contact information for both the buyer and the seller.

Specific provisions of the contract may include:

- A promise to provide ongoing and regular veterinary care including the recommended course of vaccinations.

- Agreement to meet the cat's specific grooming needs on a regular basis.

- A statement that no refund will be provided if that cat is returned for any reason.

Returns are a serious matter for breeders. The paperwork will include your agreement to a provision forbidding the giving away or selling of the cat without the breeder's permission.

Breeders are primarily concerned about the welfare of the cat. They do not want to see the animal wind up in any kind of shelter or pet store. Breeders would rather take kittens back than see that happen.

This is extremely important to emphasize. If at any point you feel that you can no longer keep the cat CONTACT THE BREEDER.

You will have to have the cat tested for ringworm, FELV/FIV, and fecal parasites before you return it, but you will always have a safe place to rehouse your cat if that proves to be necessary.

Required Spaying and Neutering

For the most part, people who work with breeders are acquiring kittens that have been judged to "pet quality". For whatever reason, the animal you are adopting is not considered a proper example of the breed for show or breeding purposes.

Don't let that concern you! You probably won't be able to recognize the flaw even if the breeder tells you what it is! You will, however, have to agree that before the baby reaches six months of age, it will be spayed or neutered.

Since this is the medically recommended period of time for either surgery to occur, this is a reasonable request by a cattery that has every right to protect its bloodlines.

The typical arrangement is that you do not receive the cat's papers until you have provided the cattery with a veterinary receipt showing that the spaying or neutering procedure has been performed.

Declawing Prohibited

Do not be surprised that the adoption agreement will expressly forbid declawing the cat in strongly worded terms. This surgery is illegal in Europe and in many parts of the United States for the simple reason that it is inhumane and completely unnecessary.

In order to remove the claw, the last digit of the cat's toe must be amputated. The procedure is painful, it affects the animal's mobility for the duration of its life, and it takes away the cat's primary means of self-defense.

Cats that have been introduced to scratching apparatus early in their life and whose claws are regularly clipped are not destructive.

Declawing is a radical measure done exclusively for the convenience of the owner and is a callous disregard of the welfare of the cat.

Known Health Conditions

In the chapter on health, I'll cover some of the medical issues associated with Birman cats, including those that are genetic in nature. You'll be glad to hear this is an extraordinarily healthy breed! Just remember that when you are adopting a pedigreed Birman, the paperwork should include a health guarantee.

There should also be a statement about the parents' health, and an indication of what evaluations and tests they have received as well as a statement of the results.

Remember that the requirement for an initial health evaluation on your part, usually within 72 hours of the time you take possession of the kitten, provides a baseline for the health guarantee. This measure protects the cat *and* you.

Preparing to Bring a Kitten Home

If you don't know it already, let me stress something that is pretty much a constant with all cats irrespective of breed — they do NOT like change. From a very early age, most cats get used to things being one way and they'd prefer that not change.

It is especially important when transitioning a kitten from a cattery to your home that everything stays the same, particularly regarding litter box arrangement and food.

Ask the breeder what kind of box the kitten has become accustomed to. You will want to know the style of the box, the height, and the kind of litter used.

Cats are very sensitive about litter texture. An abrupt change can put a cat off its box and lead to all kinds of problems. The same is true of litter box style.

I have had cats that absolutely would not use an open box under any circumstances, demanding the privacy of a covered tray.

Any changes to a cat's routine, especially in regard to the litter box, must be introduced slowly. Go in prepared to meet defeat. There may well be no more stubborn creature on the planet than a cat that has made up its mind about something.

Diet will be discussed at length in the daily care chapter, but you certainly do not want to subject a kitten to an abrupt food change. That is an open invitation for gastrointestinal upset.

Ask the breeder what the kitten has been eating and what dietary program they use with their maturing cats. Follow this advice to the letter, again, only introducing changes very slowly.

You will want to have some kitten safe toys on hand for the baby's homecoming. Don't bother with anything that has catnip. Cats show no reaction to the herb until they are 6-9 months old.

Instead, concentrate on items that do not present any kind of choking hazard. Many cat toys will always be "with supervision only" items. These include anything with strings, feathers, bells and similar attached decorations.

Get an appropriate brush for a kitten's delicate skin and start getting your baby accustomed to being brushed from the beginning of your relationship.

During seasonal changes when the cat is shedding more, additional brushing will help to minimize the development of hairballs.

Approximate Costs

A pet quality Birman kitten typically sells for $500 - $600 / £325 - £390. After that, however, the breed is no more expensive to keep than any other popular domestic cat.

They are a long-lived breed at 14-18 years with 20 years a possibility. On average, it costs $130 / £84.50 to keep a cat per month, or $1,560 / £1,014 per year.

For a complete understanding of the monthly costs associated with keeping a cat, please refer to Chapter 3 on daily care.

In the absence of a chronic illness requiring ongoing veterinary care, the bulk of your monthly expenses will be for food and litter. Approximately 75% of the amount will go directly to feeding your pet.

Never Rule Out a Rescue Cat Adoption

Obviously I'm a fan of the Birman breed or I wouldn't be writing this book. I would never discourage anyone from bringing a Birman into their home. But, like a true cat lover, my affections are not limited to pedigreed breeds.

I love all cats, including the Domestic Shorthairs often referred to as "alley cats." My first cat was a black and white tuxedo tom I named Jimmy. He was a Domestic Shorthair that grew into a wonderful, big boy who was a perfect companion for a child.

There's no doubt in my mind that my experience with him colored my perception of all the cats I've known since. I still gravitate toward toms, the bigger the better. So you see, to my mind every individual feline has unique qualities that will endear the cat to someone looking to give the animal a forever home.

This book — indeed any cat book — would be incomplete without praising the work of "no kill" shelters and rescue groups the world over. There are literally hundreds of thousands of lovely cats out there in need of a good home, and I can't say enough about the incredible people who selflessly work on their behalf.

If your heart is set on owning a Birman, you will undoubtedly have a wonderful relationship with your new pet for many years to come. But if you are simply thinking about adopting a cat, and perhaps are already a bit nervous about the cost of a pedigree pet, please don't rule out a rescue adoption.

Giving an abandoned kitten or adult cat a "forever home" is one of the greatest acts of kindness an animal lover can perform, one for which you will be rewarded daily with the love and loyalty of an animal that might very well have died otherwise.

Check your local shelter and speak with your veterinarian to find rescue groups in your area. I assure you, there will be many. Trap/neuter/release programs work hard every day to stem the raging epidemic of unwanted stray animals, but it is still an epic and tragic problem.

If you do move forward with your plans to adopt a pedigree Birman, please remember the efforts of rescue groups with your kind donations. These endeavors are always underfunded and understaffed. They need your help, but more importantly, the cats need your help!

Human Health Considerations

Before you buy you also need to consider any implications to your own health. For example, do you know if you have an allergy or sensitivity to cats? I would recommend taking advice from your Doctor to ensure that you understand the implications to your own health and if necessary, are allergy tested.

Chapter 3 – Daily Care for Your Cat

The basics of cat care are fairly standard for most breeds, with obvious differences for short and long-haired cats, or even for those, like the Sphinx, that have virtually no hair at all.

A great deal of successful feline husbandry involves understanding life from the perspective of your cat. In the case of the Birman, you are starting your relationship with your new pet with a distinct advantage.

One of the reasons this breed is so popular is that Birmans tend to be wonderfully easy going cats with almost no fussy tendencies.

Personality notwithstanding, there are some standard precautions when bringing a Birman kitten into the household. All kittens think they're Bengal tigers and they can get into Bengal tiger-sized trouble fast!

The Need to "Kitten Proof"

Many people underestimate kittens for the simple reason that they are small — or at least you think they are until one gallops over you in the night or goes thundering down the hall.

Take basic steps to "kitten proof" your home like removing potentially toxic houseplants, taping cords and wires to the baseboards, capping electrical outlets, and securing or moving large heavy objects that could get pulled down or knocked over.

Fortunately, the breed is not destructive by nature. The problem with kittens — and this is true of any breed, not just Birmans — is that they have zero judgment.

Kitten proofing the house, in this case, is much more about protecting your new little baby than taking care of your stuff. A good place to start is having a look at your houseplants and what you have growing outside.

Beware of Toxic Houseplants

Like many breeds, Birmans are often tempted to start nibbling on houseplants. This bad habit is a double edged sword. You may not enjoy the destruction of your plants, but you must also realize that many houseplants are actually quite toxic to cats.

The Cat Fancier's Association has produced a fairly comprehensive list of the most hazardous plants and it is always better to be overly cautious with vegetation and plant life. Of this lot, lilies are especially dangerous.

I appreciate it can be difficult to monitor and physically do anything about neighboring properties but any of the plants on this list should be kept strictly away from cats, and your pet should not be allowed into the garden if you have these items growing there or in your yard.

If your Birman eats any part of a plant you believe to be poisonous, seek the help of a qualified veterinarian immediately.

In Appendix 2, I have itemized this list as I think it is an important resource and I hope you will find it of assistance and reassurance in respect of the plants you may have growing in your garden or yard.

Making an Easy Transition

The best advice on helping your Birman kitten make a smooth transition to life with you will come directly from the breeder.

This breed has many things going for it in terms of adaptability. Birmans tend to take most everything in stride, including dogs and other cats. They have a resilient disposition that serves them well if there are children in the house.

As your cat ages, he should grow into an easygoing companion with a steady nature. Birmans are not nervous, and they don't tend to overreact. Still, however, you will be bringing home a very young cat.

No matter how big a kitten *thinks* he is, he's still a tiny little fellow and coming to live with you means he's leaving everything and everyone he knows. The more you can cushion this transition, the better.

At first, you will want to keep your new pet confined to a relatively contained area, or a completely segregated space if there are other cats in the house.

The best initial introductions with other pets are those conducted via the "sniff test" through a closed bedroom or bathroom door. This generally leads to a little exploratory under-the-door paw play as well.

Face-to-face introductions should always be supervised, but do not intervene unless it's absolutely necessary. Animals will pick up on our emotions. If you are nervous, they will be nervous.

Do not overreact, and if a "rescue" is necessary, just quickly and quietly pick up the kitten and return it to its own "room" until you're ready to try again.

Most cats need about a week to 10 days to become fully acclimatized to new surroundings. That's about the same length of time necessary for the hierarchy to get worked out in multiple pet households.

Don't be surprised if your kitten shoots to the top of that "pecking order". They can be veritable little tyrants, and those tiny claws are very, very sharp.

The Mind of a Cat

It's a commonly held belief that understanding the thought processes of a cat is next to impossible. Your Birman will gaze up at you with those phenomenal azure eyes and you'll fall completely under his spell – all the while knowing that you'll never be able to completely fathom what's going on in that agile feline mind.

In truth, however, the majority of the stereotypes people entertain about cats are completely wrong. While some breeds are more reserved than others, that factor is more an individual trait than a genetic standard. Cats aren't nearly so inscrutable as popular wisdom would have you believe.

It is not uncommon for a cat to single out one person for special affection. While they may be friendly to others in the family, they will lavish their love, loyalty, and attention on their favorite. Birmans can go either way with this trait, but even when they do pick a special person, it's not to the complete exclusion of other members of the family.

Cats are not the self-sufficient loners of the animal world people make them out to be. Some cats will do fine on their own during the day, but they will want your attention at night, even greeting you at the door to hear about your day. Birmans certainly fall into that category.

When you bring a pet of any kind into your life, you're not just responsible for its care and feeding in a physical sense. You must also meet your pet's emotional needs.

Most behavior problems stem from an animal that is simply not getting enough attention. Cats get lonely, bored, and unhappy, and they let you know about it in the only ways that are available to them.

We tend to think of things like furniture shredding or knocking things over as a cat being "bad". In reality, those instances are examples of a cat trying to tell you something.

The one situation that absolutely makes me see red, and that I will write about at greater length later in this chapter, occurs when people turn their cats over to shelters due to poor litter box habits.

If you were to go into the home and look at the litter box, in 9 out of 10 cases, it will be filthy. Cats are fastidious creatures with a highly acute and well developed sense of smell. They won't go in a urine-soaked box, and they have definite preferences in regard to litter texture and box design.

Even more serious, however, is the very real possibility that a cat that is going outside of the box has an undiagnosed kidney or bladder condition.

If a cat attempts to urinate in the box and experiences pain, it associates the discomfort with the location. The poor thing is just trying to find a place to go without hurting!

If you are a first-time cat owner, don't fall for such ridiculous and cruel stereotypes. The more you are engaged in your pet's day-to-day life, the better you will understand his language, and the better you can anticipate problems before they occur.

I have owned cats for more than 40 years and can attest to the unique qualities of each as an individual irrespective of breed. The important thing is that you spend time with your pet and learn how he communicates.

I love a Birman's capacity for wordless "conversations." Like other Oriental breeds, they have terrific intuition and powers of observation, correctly zeroing in on subtle nuances of mood.

Many dog people are quite taken aback to hear that cats know and care when their people have had a bad day, but it's true. Don't be at all surprised to find your Birman snuggled up beside you offering comfort when you come home emotionally bruised from a lousy day on the job.

Birmans, unlike some breeds, are not completely wedded to routine. They are adaptable, and won't throw a fit if every activity isn't accomplished in the same order every day. Also, since they aren't prone to weight gain, you can leave food out for them and not have to deal with wailed assurances that your cat is starving to death the instant you walk in the door.

I actually think cats are quite clear in the ways in which they communicate with us; they simply deliver their messages differently than dogs.

Canines are a more effusive species, but cats still get their meaning across quite clearly if you know how to read their body language, facial expressions, and vocal intonations.

Dietary and Nutritional Information

Your emphasis in selecting foods for your cat should always be on quality. Based on the advice you initially receive from your breeder, and then from your veterinarian, buy the best food you can afford.

The following information and guidelines will help you to further refine the choices you make to optimize your cat's nutritional intake.

Wet or Dry?

This is the initial question most pet owners' face. The tendency is all too often to go with dry due to the convenience both in serving the food, and in the belief that using dry food will make litter box maintenance easier.

This is a mistake. Cats are carnivores. Wet food provides them with a vital source of hydration, and cats that are fed canned food are less prone to gain weight than those that receive dry food only.

The best choice for your Birman is to feed a healthy mixture of wet and dry food that provides not only the correct mixture of nutrients, but also the tastes and textures your pet will enjoy.

A Note on Weight

Before we discuss actually choosing foods, let me give you a quick tip on how to judge the shape of your cat's figure.

If you stand over your cat and look down at his body while he is also standing, you should be able to see a slight indentation just behind the rib cage.

This is an excellent sign that your cat's weight is being maintained at a healthy level. If you can't see any "hips," Fluffy is probably getting a little too heavy.

Don't ever let your cats get started on human food. Many of the things we eat simply aren't good for our feline friends (more on that in just a minute), but giving a cat human food is an invitation to health problems.

Once a cat starts to become overweight, it's just a small step to conditions like diabetes, heart problems and joint diseases. Cats are skilled beggars. Use your will power! Don't fall down that slippery slope.

Dangerous "People" Foods

There are many things that we eat every day that a cat should never touch due to their toxicity in the feline system. These items include, but are not limited to:

- alcoholic beverages
- avocados
- grapes / raisins
- eggs
- garlic
- onions
- chives
- yeast dough
- caffeine in any form
- chocolate

The toxic elements present in chocolate are substances called methylxanthines, which are found in cacao seeds. A similar extract is used in soda beverages, which a cat should never be allowed to consume.

Cats that have been exposed to chocolate or to sodas can exhibit symptoms that are severe to the point of being life threatening. These may include:

- excessive thirst
- panting
- vomiting
- diarrhea
- irregular heartbeat
- seizures
- tremors

Sodas also contain sweeteners that include xylitol, which can cause liver failure in cats. Err on the safe side, and keep your pet away from all sweet items.

Salty foods are equally dangerous as they can cause rapid dehydration, creating a serious health risk.

Cats and Milk

Although milk is not necessarily toxic to cats, it's also not the be all and end all of the feline diet as many people believe. A large percentage of cats are as lactose intolerant as their human keepers.

Felines do not produce sufficient amounts of the enzyme lactase. This means they do not efficiently digest cow's milk and are subject to gastrointestinal upset and diarrhea if they are given too much dairy content in their diets.

Adult cats do not require milk and they actually don't get a lot of nutritional value from consuming it. All mammals produce milk that is correct for their own young, and, to state the obvious, cats aren't cows.

You can certainly offer your cat milk or cream occasionally as a treat, but if there is any sign of stomach upset or discomfort, discontinue the practice.

Reading Labels

When you read the label of a food you are considering for your pet, never lose sight of the fact that cats are meat eaters. If the first item on the label is not meat, look at another food.

As a general rule, the cheaper foods contain much more plant material as filler, while the more expensive or premium foods have a greater amount of meat.

There are so many kinds of cat food on the market it's best to go with breeder and veterinarian recommendations and your own budget in making a specific selection.

Estimating Food Costs

With the great variety of foods on the market, offering a clear estimate of food costs is all but impossible. Conservatively, and based entirely on my own experience, you will likely spend $50 / £32.50 each month on wet food with $25 / £16.25 going for dry in the same period.

Birmans are not prone to over-eating, so you can follow a practice of free feeding which is making dry food available at all times with no fear that your pet will become overweight.

I do recommend that you try to limit the amount of dry food to a quarter to half a cup per day or 2 to 4 ounces / 56.7 to 113 grams. Most Birmans won't eat more than this anyway, and rationing the amount will keep the dry food from going stale.

Put out wet food once to twice per day. These servings should be roughly 5.5 ounces / 156 grams each.

Food and Water Bowls

For the most part you will be able to use plain bowls for both food and water, but you do need to be aware of a potential sensitivity called "whisker stress".

Some cats do not like the feeling of their whiskers dragging against the side of a bowl. You can tell that this is happening if your pet routinely picks up food and drops it on the floor to eat it.

Try switching to a receptacle that is more like a tray to cut down on the irritating sensation for your pet. There are products made specifically for cats for this purpose.

Normal food and water bowls will each cost $5 - $10 / £3.25 - £6.50. Try to use either stainless steel or crockery as plastic has a tendency to cause a breaking out on cat's chins that is commonly referred to as feline acne.

If you do opt for a bowl designed to reduce whisker stress, you will spend about $25 / £16.25. These trays typically come with legs or a stand to make them more stable and are thus slightly more expensive.

Be sure that your cat has a constant supply of clean drinking water. Some cats far prefer to drink running water, and I am a big fan of feline water fountains. These units sell for $30 / £19.50.

The Raw Diet Considered

Many pet owners over the past few years have been attracted to the idea of giving their pets, both dogs and cats the "raw" diet. The idea is to provide the animals with the kind of nutritional intake they would receive if they were hunting on their own.

Please understand that I mention this here not to advocate the diet or to instruct you in the proper administration of this dietary program. If you are interested in "feeding raw," you must research this topic thoroughly and discuss it with your veterinarian. Be prepared to hear serious reservations.

The majority of veterinarians and many cat experts do not believe that the raw concept is a good one since it includes bones. Even ground, bone shards can severely lacerate a cat's throat and intestines.

This, and the risk of salmonella poisoning, makes raw feeding for cats a questionable proposition. Certainly there is much more to this process than simply putting raw meat in your cat's bowl.

If you are interested in raw feeding, you have to learn how to do it, and you have to have the correct equipment. Strict standards of sanitation must be met, and only raw beef and chicken can be used.

All uneaten food, even if it has been refrigerated, must be discarded after 2-3 days and none of the food can ever be microwaved.

Just because your cat is a carnivore by nature, do not feel that a raw diet is necessary and do not proceed with such a feeding program without expert advice and adequate research.

Managing the Litter Box

In the beginning use the type of box to which the kitten has become accustomed at the breeder's. Also use the same kind of litter.

Any time you decide to try a different box or litter type, always leave the original arrangement in place until you know your cat will use the new option.

If your cat does go outside the box, you must clean the area with special enzymatic cleaners like those produced by Nature's Miracle $5 - $10 / £3.25 - £6.50.

Cats interpret the world as a complex mix of smells. Any time your cat has urinated or defecated on a spot, and can still detect the scents he has left there, he may well consider that place acceptable to do his "business".

Picking a Litter

Whereas once the only commercially available litter was standard clay gravel, there are now many choices for cat owners to consider.

Clay Gravel

Clay gravel remains the tried and true traditional approach and it is also the cheapest. You can purchase 10 lbs. / 4.54 kg of this material for as little as $2.50 - $5.00 / £1.66 - £3.25.

The major drawback with clay gravel is the amount of dust it produces, and its low capacity to absorb moisture and control odor.

Clumping Sand

Clumping sand has become one of the most popular litters on the market. While it also generates dust, and has a capacity to fly all over the place if you have a cat who likes to dig, clumping litters have much better odor and moisture control.

Remember, if you are using a clumping litter, do not flush the clumps unless the mixture specifically says, "flushable". Regular clumping litter will absolutely destroy your plumbing, essentially turning to concrete in your pipes.

Clumping litter is more expensive than clay, but it is available in large amounts, for instance, 42 lbs. / 19.51 kg for $18 / £11.70.

Multiple cat mixes or those that claim extra odor controlling properties may be extremely pricey, however, with only 1.4 lbs. / 0.63 kg retailing for as much as $30 / £19.50.

"Green" Litters

Cat litters that are plant-based are generally made of materials like pine. They can be cost effective and are certainly environmentally friendly, but not all cats will use them.

Because the shavings are so lightweight, some cats don't seem to think they "feel" right. Never underestimate how sensitive cats are to texture, in many areas of their lives.

If your cat will use green litters, you will pay around $10 / £6.50 for 30 lbs. / 13.61 kg.

Absorbing Crystals

Crystals are the latest innovation in cat litters, and are touted for their ability to cut down on the potential for bacterial growth. The silica gel from which the crystals are made traps urine and holds it, allowing for a dry box and easier clean up.

Again, this is a matter of texture for the cat's paws. Not all cats will use crystals, and they are expensive, albeit effective. On average, 8 lbs. / 3.63 kg of absorbing crystals sells for $16 / £10.40.

Picking a Box

After you have made your choice of litter type, you must consider what kind of box to offer your cat. Again, in the beginning, use what the kitten thinks is "normal" based on its experience at the cattery.

Your major options in this area start with the tried and true open pan. This is a cheap avenue at just $6 - $10 / £3.90 - £6.50, but there are drawbacks.

Open pans allow cats who like to scratch to fling litter far and wide, and they are a nightmare when it comes to dust control.

Many cats don't like open pans because they don't care to be watched. Additionally, open pans are unsightly. Homeowners have to find some place to both hide the pan and make it accessible to the cat, which can be a challenge.

Covered boxes answer many of these issues, giving the cat privacy, and hiding the mess. Since the lids are typically outfitted with a filter, a covered box will cut down on both dust and odor.

Depending on the size and shape of the box (square, rectangular, round, or triangular to fit in corners), you will spend $30 - $50 / £19.50 - £32.50 for a covered litter box.

The latest innovation is the self-scooping box, which humans love and cats treat with either a certain amount of fascination, suspicion or open horror.

Self-scooping boxes require electricity since they employ a scoop activated by a motion sensor that is tripped when the cat exits the pan. The scoop rakes through the litter, depositing the soiled material in a closed receptacle.

When the receptacle is full, simply cap it with a provided lid and throw it away, putting a fresh disposable refill in its place.

If your cat does not react with fear to the mechanism, this can be an excellent solution for cat owners who are weary of scooping. This kind of automated arrangement costs approximately $150 - $200 / £97.50 - £130.

Be warned. If you decide to try a self-scooping box, keep your old pan in place. Fluffy may well rebel at this idea and demand his old "out house" back.

The Birman at Play

Birmans are not as relentlessly active as some breeds. A Bengal, for instance, will fairly wear you out! Birmans can be seriously playful, but they like to intersperse their active phases with some nice napping and lap time, which makes for an excellent mix for their humans.

Birmans are one of the cat breeds that will engage in games of "fetch," and they are especially fond of batting around balls and even crumpled up paper wads. Small toys seem to work very well for this breed – anything that can be tossed up in the air and batted about.

Unlike some of their Oriental cousins, Birmans are not vigorous or destructive scratchers, so a simple carpeted scratching pole retailing for $30 / £19.50 will do nicely for this breed.

However, pretty much any cat will love it if you sell out $100 - $300 / £65 - £195 for an elaborate cat tree outfitted with platforms, tunnels, perches, and ramps. Arrangements like that seem to bring out the "jungle beast" in almost any cat.

If your Birman does show an unhealthy interest in your furniture, you can discourage this behavior with pennyroyal or orange essence sprays at $12 - $15 / £7.80 - £9.75 or double-side adhesive strips at $8 - $10 / £5.20 - £6.50.

Speaking Cat

Often Birman owners say that they expect their cats to speak to them at any time. There's something about the way a Birman gazes at you with those lovely round eyes that seems to suggest he's about to talk. The truth? He's already speaking, but you may not be listening.

Cats have a complex language that is built not just on vocalizations, but also on facial expression and body language. Most people think, for instance, that when a cat rubs up against his human, it's an expression of affection. Try "ownership".

When your cat is rubbing up against you, he's using the scent glands located around his mouth to mark you as his territory. Now, granted, you may have "most favored nation" status, but the rubbing has pretty much the same purpose whether it's you or the edge of the coffee table.

When a cat leans into you with his whole weight or "bonks" you with his head, this is more of an expression of camaraderie and affection - and likely a request for an ear scratching or a chin rub. This is the same message a cat is sending when he positions himself between you and the laptop screen or plops down on your book.

Some other bits of body language that are clear messages if you know how to read them include:

- Picking up a paw and shaking it with an expression of disgust because that's exactly what the cat is saying. "I don't like how this feels, smells or tastes. Yuck!"

- Lashing the tail about. Surely you know this one! A cat with a lashing tail is not happy, to the point of being actively peeved. This is especially so if your pet's ears are back and his eyes are narrowed; let him have some time to calm down.

- Holding the tail straight up. This is the best expression of a feline good mood you can see. That tail might as well be a flag emblazoned with the word, "Happy!"

- Holding the tail straight out from the body. Think of this one as lowering the flag a bit. Now the message is, "Hmm. I'm not sure about this". Your cat isn't yet in a bad mood, but he's definitely checking the temperature of things.

- Holding the tail down. Now the flag has been run down the pole. Your cat is not happy, and he's likely exiting the room. A tail held down can indicate fear, or unease with the situation. A cat that has just broken a flower pot won't apologize, but he's smart enough to know you're not going to be thrilled with him, so being elsewhere is, in his mind, a great idea.

While many of these cues are universal to all cats, remember that every cat is an individual. The real way to "get" your cat's message is just cultivating familiarity over long association. Most cat owners don't need interpreters to know what their cat is saying or to figure out the opinion their pet is expressing.

All dyed in the wool cat people know, "the look," which is usually delivered with withering proficiency right after you've put something sub-standard in kitty's bowl. "The look" is a commentary on human intelligence, and we don't rate well in that moment!

Grooming Requirements

Tangles and mats are one of the biggest concerns in maintaining a longhaired cat's coat, but the lack of an undercoat in the Birman mitigates this issue.

Unlike a longhaired Persian, you will not need to brush your Birman daily. A weekly combing to remove loose hairs is typically sufficient.

Shedding combs have a combination of long and short wire teeth in alternating rows and work extremely well with this breed. The combs retail for $10 / £6.50 or less.

Claw Clipping

Claw clipping generally can be done safely at home, and is always the first step in a professional grooming session. To complete this chore safely:

- Place your Birman on your lap.
- Pick up one front paw.
- Apply gentle pressure with your thumb behind the toes.
- With the claws extended, examine the nail.
- The claw is translucent.
- The vascular "quick" is pink.
- Snip off only the clear tips.
- Do not forget the dewclaw on the side of the foot.

Be extremely careful not to nip the "quick" as this will not only cause your pet pain, but result in profuse bleeding.

Try not to hold your cat down. "Less restraint" is better because no cat likes to feel trapped. With practice, you can safely and quickly trim your pet's nails before the cat even realizes what is happening but I've found Birmans to be fairly compliant with claw clipping.

Buy clippers specifically designed for pets. Those with plier grips are easy to use and offer superior control. They are priced at approximately $10 / £6.50.

If you are in any way nervous about doing this, it would be a wise precaution to ask your vet to show you how to trim your cats nails on the first occasion.

Testing Your Cat's Tolerance

For many people the idea of giving a cat a bath sounds like a recipe for disaster. Frankly, it can be, but generally Birmans are good about this process, especially if they've been introduced to bathing from an early age.

While it is rare for a Birman kept as a pet to need a bath, accidents do happen. Certainly show cats will need to be very accustomed to a complete grooming regimen.

With any cat you are attempting to bathe, you may want to try the "tail test." If you put your cat's tail in the water and the animal goes ballistic, then you know that a professional groomer is going to have to take over.

The same method will work with the blow dryer. Turn the unit on once and you'll know in about 2 seconds how your Birman is going to feel about the "monster."

If you are bathing your Birman at home on your own, a blow dryer isn't an absolute necessity. You can towel dry the cat, so long as you don't scrub at the fur, which can cause tangling.

Dry in the condition the fur lies. Hold the cat wrapped in a towel to prevent it from getting cold. As the fur dries, you can use a comb to further mitigate the chance of snarls forming.

The Actual Bath

If your Birman is agreeable and you go ahead with the bath, assemble all of your supplies and have them close by. The last thing you want to do is turn loose of a wet cat! Keep the bath water lukewarm, but no hotter.

Don't let water get in your pet's ears, eyes, or nose. Although not all cats will stand for it, soft cotton balls tucked just inside the ear are a good precaution.

Do not ever pour water over the cat's face. Instead, clean this area with a warm washcloth. Do not use soap around your pet's eyes.

Using Shampoo

Always use a hypoallergenic, natural shampoo on your cat. These products sell in a price range of $10 - $15 / £6.50 - £9.75 for 16 ounces / 454 grams.

Be very gentle when applying the shampoo. Don't scrub, as this action will cause tangling. Rinse repeatedly so as to leave no residue in the coat.

When the shampoo is out of the coat, drain the sink or tub. Run your hands through the cat's fur in a straight, downward motion to get as much excess water out of the fur as possible.

Wrap your pet in a soft, dry towel and use the same kind of even strokes to continue drying the hair. Again, avoid any "scrubbing" action.

Clipping and Trimming Fur

It is not a good idea to trim or clip your Birman's fur at home. The risk of seriously hurting your pet is too great. In warmer regions, many longhaired cats receive a "lion cut."

The body is shaved, with a "mane" at the neck and "cuffs" at the ankles left in place. This approach can give your cat relief from summer heat.

Attending to Eye Care

Although tearing is not as common with Birmans as with other breeds like the Persian, any cat can be plagued with this problem and with the attendant facial staining.

In order to clean your cat's face, use a foam cosmetic disc dipped in warm water. Gently wipe at the corner of the cat's eyes with a soft, downward motion. You can use the same method for any nasal drainage present.

Since both tearing and nasal drainage can be a sign of seasonal allergies or a respiratory infection, consult your veterinarian if this problem lasts more than a day or so.

Caring for the Ears

Ear care really should be left to a professional groomer or to your veterinarian. If you see black, tarry debris on the ear or just inside the ear, you can softly clean the area with a cotton ball dipped in warm water. Do not ever insert a cotton swab in the ear canal.

Excessive thick, tarry debris and a yeasty smell indicates the presence of ear mites, necessitating a visit to the veterinarian.

Evaluating Professional Groomers

Birmans, like many pedigreed cats, may benefit from the occasional professional grooming, but this is not a hard and fast requirement of ownership and care.

Under the best circumstances, you will be able to find a groomer who will come to your home. Very few cats of any breed like to be taken out of their familiar environment. Cats are always calmer when everything around them is "theirs."

Ask your breeder for references for local groomers, and inquire at your vet clinic. Most practices keep a bulletin board in the waiting room where groomers and pet sitters leave their flyers or business cards.

Always visit a grooming facility or interview a groomer before booking an appointment for your pet. You want to see how the animals are secured against escape and ensure that the place is clean and well maintained.

Specifically ensure that the establishment requires all client animals to be current with their vaccinations. Feline diseases are highly contagious, so the cats should be kept strictly separated while on the premises.

Grooming costs can vary rather widely, but typically a single session will cost approximately $50 / £30.64.

Time Away from Your Cat

All pet owners face one common concern: What happens when it is time to go on vacation? Many people travel with their pets, but the fact is pets cannot always go with their families. What will you do with your cat when you have to go away from home – on vacation or out of town for business or for a funeral, for example?

Consider who will look after your cat before the need ever arises. You have several options. Perhaps a friend or a family member, who has been around your cat and feels comfortable, can call to your home to care for it.

Pet sitters are also a popular option, especially in the United States where pet sitting businesses must be licensed and insured to operate. A pet sitter generally comes to your home to visit your pet – to ensure he has food, water, and time out to exercise. Pet sitters typically charge per visit, and you can schedule several visits each day.

Is a pet sitter a viable option for your cat? That depends. How long will you be gone? Can you afford to have the pet sitter come each day to ensure your cat is looked after as you wish? Be sure, if you look for a pet sitter, to find someone who has experience caring for cats. Before you hire a pet sitter or agree to a visiting schedule, the pet sitter will generally come to your home for an initial consultation. During that meeting, you will talk with the pet sitter about your cat, its schedule, diet, and any other concern you may have. But, more importantly, the meeting will allow your cat and the pet sitter to meet and to become comfortable around each other. Some pet sitters charge for this initial meeting, but many do not.

You can find pet sitters in the United States through the National Association of Pet Sitters (www.petsitters.org) and Pet Sitters International (www.petsit.com). A comprehensive list of pet sitters in the United Kingdom can be found through the National Association of Registered Pet Sitters (www.dogsit.com) and yes, they look after more than dogs and don't have any trouble with cats!

Make sure that your pet sitter is insured and fully referenced as they will have access to you home and your pet. You should also contact your home insurance providers to confirm your cover is not affected by having a pet sitter stay at your home.

If you do not like the idea of a pet sitter, then some rescue organizations offer boarding and pet sitting services while others may just be able to provide you with recommendations of sitters.

If you have trouble finding someone you trust or don't want to become a burden to family and friends then you may want to consider boarding.

Boarding Your Birman

If it should prove necessary to board your Birman while you are away or due to other life circumstances, you'll find that your pet will tend to react to the experience with his usual aplomb.

These cats really are rather unflappable, which is one of the attractions to the breed. In all likelihood, you will be much more nervous than your cat! If your regular veterinarian does not offer boarding services, here are some guidelines to help you choose a boarding facility:

- Begin checking out facilities well in advance of your trip, especially if it coincides with a major holiday. These places fill up quickly.

- If possible, find a boarder that caters to cats only or that keep their feline clients well segregated from dogs and other pets. Cats like quiet, especially when they are in an unfamiliar place.

- Make sure that your pet's food and water intake is closely monitored, especially in the first 24-48 hours. Cats can become dehydrated quickly when they are stressed, which can lead to serious health problems.

- If there is a health problem, does the facility have a vet on staff and what provisions can be made for that person to immediately contact your cat's regular vet?

- Will your cat require any vaccinations or boosters before being allowed to board at the establishment? Do you need to supply any medical records prior to the stay?

- Make sure that your cat will be housed in a spacious enclosure alone. Cats, unlike dogs, do not want to mingle. Additionally, many feline diseases are highly transmittable by nothing more than a nose tap.

- If you have more than one cat and will be boarding both, make sure they will be allowed to remain together in the same enclosure.

Be sure to schedule a time to tour the facility. Ask for references, and discuss the facility you are considering with your veterinarian. Always transport your cat in a secure cat carrier. Never allow your pet to ride in the car unless it is inside its crate, which should be securely locked.

Coming Home Again

How will your cat react when you return home, especially if you have been gone a considerable period? Well, cats are like people, so do not be surprised if your beloved friend is angry with you for having left them. And, like people, he will need time to shed that anger. On the other hand, cats while being extremely independent may just give you a look that says "Oh it's you!" and then won't leave your side for days in case you disappear again.

Chapter 4 – Senior Moments

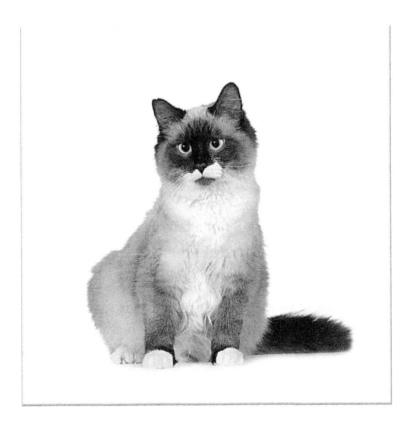

Not all cats age the same way, any more than all humans experience the same age-related problems. I have had cats with arthritis, one that went blind, and others that developed benign fatty tumors called lipomas.

The signs of aging tend to be gradual. Some of the most typical are included in this chapter.

Less Acute Senses

You may begin to notice subtle signs that your cat is not hearing or seeing as well as it once did. These changes may, however, completely escape your attention.

Some years ago one of my senior cats who went blind compensated so well that I had no idea anything was wrong until I rearranged the living room furniture.

Her obvious confusion led me to schedule a vet visit and we discovered that not only was she blind, but that she was suffering from high blood pressure and needed medication.

Obviously no cat that has vision or hearing loss should ever be allowed outdoors. I am not a fan of "outside" cats anyway, as our modern world is far too dangerous for our beloved pets.

Frankly, I would be more concerned about your cat's senses of smell and taste. Deficits with these two abilities can adversely affect your pet's appetite and lead to weight loss. Cats won't eat what they can't smell, so it may be necessary to alter an older cat's diet.

Consult with your vet first so that you don't give a senior cat something that will cause gastrointestinal upset. If your cat isn't used to eating "fishy" foods, they may like the smell, but get an upset tummy from the richer fare.

You can try just slightly warming your pet's existing wet food to increase the smell, but be very careful not to get it too hot. If you warm the food in the microwave, stir it well with a fork and let it cool to just slightly more than room temperature before you give it to your cat. Please ensure that any uneaten food is thrown away quickly to avoid the risk of bacterial growth and the food spoiling.

Changes in Appearance

It's perfectly normal for cats to lose muscle mass as they age, but always have any dramatic changes in weight, both losses and gains evaluated by your veterinarian.

Also pay close attention to the condition of an aging cat's coat. If your pet is not able to groom as well as he once did, you may need to step in and help with more frequent brushing.

Since the Birman's coat is thick and silky, be especially mindful about any thinning or matting. Both are signs of potential bad health.

Cats can develop arthritis the same way humans do and your pet may simply not be able to reach the hard spots any more. This may extend to "personal" areas. Without annoying your cat, just make sure all is well under the tail. If cleaning there is necessary, gently use a warm washcloth and plain, clean water. Please ensure that you observe good hand hygiene and wash the cloth between uses.

Make sure the litter box is low enough for your pet to get in and out of easily. Since cats don't like changes in box type or litter consistency, consider trimming down the front edge of the box so your pet can step in and out more easily.

Changes in Mood and Behavior

The most important thing to do with a senior citizen cat is to be aware of subtle changes in mood and behavior. An older cat may no longer be able to jump up to the window sill, but would still like to sun. Give him a way to "stair step" to his favorite perch without jumping.

Birmans have mellow dispositions and become more so as senior citizens. All older cats tend to spend more time sleeping, and it can be quite difficult to distinguish this type of normal slowing down from actual illness.

Always remember that cats instinctively hide their pain and illness. Use your judgment and your understanding of your pet's nature. Never hesitate to schedule a vet visit. I always give the same advice, "If you think something is wrong with your cat, it probably is".

The last thing you need to worry about is being labeled a "crazy cat lady" or a "doting Dad". You know your pet better than anyone. Go with your gut, especially when it comes to older cats. Make the vet appointment if you think your cat is sick or just not doing well.

Regular Checkups

Make sure your older cat has regular checkups. Seniors are more likely to develop dental issues, and all skin growths should be evaluated.

Monitor changes in litter box habits that might signal a urinary tract infection or more serious kidney problems. If the cat is vomiting more than usual, a vet visit may be in order.

Drinking large amounts of water might indicate the presence of diabetes Aging cats can also suffer from hyperthyroidism and high blood pressure, both of which are very treatable.

Because older cats sleep more, they are more prone to be cold. Make sure your senior has a warm bed and lots of quiet time. The warmth will also help if your pet is suffering from arthritis.

Treat your aging cats like what they are, little ladies and old gents with fur. Love them all the same, and make whatever changes you need to in their environment to keep them happy, engaged, and comfortable in their golden years.

Making the Hard Decision

Saying good-bye to a beloved companion of many years is both heartbreaking and a great act of love. Euthanasia is a difficult topic, both for you to read about and for me to write about.

I can only share with you what I believe to be the truth based on my personal experience. No one can tell you when it is time to make the hard decision but your cat.

Do not listen to anyone who makes you feel pressured to come to a decision. I promise you that you would resent this in the future if you do so.

Get the best medical information that you can from your veterinarian, conduct your own research, and simply be with your cat. I cared for a well-loved pet through a 25-month struggle with cancer.

The people in my life knew better than to try to offer advice. My veterinarian was kind, professional and honest. I will admit I spent money on treatments and medications I could not afford for the simple reason that my pet was enjoying his life and was still very much himself.

The day that he was not, he told me so. Only an "animal person" may understand what I mean, but I assure you my cat told me it was time to go. When he did, I called the vet and we gently and lovingly, helped him through that transition.

I have observed euthanasia from the perspective of a breaking heart. I can tell you with great certainty that when performed by caring, understanding veterinary professionals this is the ultimate act of compassion. My vet had a relationship both with my pet and with me.

She remains my good friend and I will always be grateful to her for the care she gave my feline companion to the very last moment of his life.

I cannot stress enough how important it is for you as a pet owner to have a vet with whom you can work in this way. I know this experience would have been truly horrible had I been dealing with a vet who did not understand both my cat's illness and my own emotional pain.

In the aftermath, allow yourself to grieve. You may have to find other "animal people" who will truly understand the loss you are suffering, but be assured that it is a valid loss of a living creature that has been part of your life and a member of your family.

The kindest thing anyone said to me as I struggled to keep my composure in the days following my pet's death was simply, "I am so sorry you lost your friend".

Our pets give us unconditional love, even when we are not being our best selves. The absence of that constancy is a deep loss and one that neither you nor anyone in your life should attempt to minimize.

Adopting a Senior Cat

People who adopt grown cats in need, especially seniors are, in my estimation very special angels. Many lovely older pets are put down every year when all they need is a loving second home.

You will be taking in an animal with established habits and preferences, and likely pre-existing needs, but there is no reason to think you cannot have a loving relationship with an older animal in its golden years.

If you are prepared to meet the special needs of a senior cat, including late in life veterinary expenses, giving an older, homeless cat a home is a vital part of feline rescue work. This is an area of that mission that always needs more willing volunteers.

Chapter 5 – Birman Cat Health

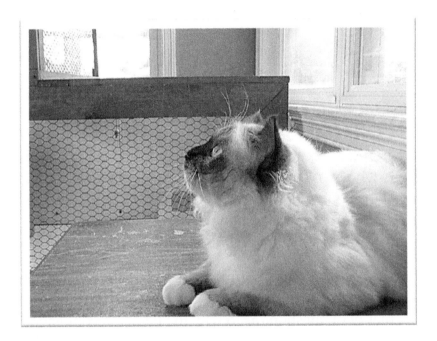

Ongoing preventive health care is the greatest medical service you can provide for your Birman. Think of yourself as your cat's primary health "insurance." The longer you live with your cat, the more you will know what is "normal" for your Birman.

One of the best pieces of advice cat owners can take to heart is this: if you think something is wrong with your pet, then something probably is. Never hesitate to take a companion animal to the vet for fear of being perceived as an over-protective "parent".

Cats hide sickness and pain for as long as they possibly can. This behavior is part of their survival instinct. As small carnivores, they have an innate awareness of their place in the food chain.

In the wild, the appearance of weakness increases the chance of potential predation from larger animals. Even the safest house cat cannot overcome the power of that instinct.

Finding a Vet

Sometimes the best way to find a great local vet is to ask others who own cats. If you do not know someone in your neighborhood with a cat, contact your local animal rescue or go online and find an online discussion group in your area and start asking for recommendations.

In addition to helping you find a good, qualified vet, other cat owners can help you avoid the not-so-desirable vets. Ask plenty of questions as to why the person recommends the particular vet. Is the vet personable and knowledgeable about cats in general? Does he or she have experience? Are his or her prices reasonable, in the person's opinion? Find out as much as you can as to why the person likes the vet. Also ask them what they do not like about the vet.

The Basics of Preventive Health Care

While interacting with your cat on a daily basis, be aware of all the following signs of potential illness and follow up with a vet should any of these symptoms or behavioral changes appear in your Birman.

Changes in weight.

This can mean either a gain or a loss. Cats with a healthy weight have a pad of fat over the ribs, but the bones can still be felt through this layer. Looking down at the cat, you should be able to see an indentation behind the rib cage where the "hips" start.

Physical changes in gait including a reluctance to perform certain motions like running or jumping.

Essentially when a cat displays these kinds of "favoring" behaviors, there is a strong chance the animal is experiencing joint or muscle pain, or that a growth is inhibiting normal movement.

Differences in the level of moisture on the nose.

This can extend to either a dry nose or an actual runny nose indicating the presence of a cold or an infection. A cat's nose under normal circumstances should be clean and dry, but not cracked. There should be no discharge from the nostrils, either clear or discolored.

Presence of discharge from the eyes.

All cats occasionally get an accumulation of "matter" in the eyes, but you should consult your vet if it is excessive and/or persistent. Always make sure the pupils of the eyes are equal and centered and that the whites are not discolored and have only minimal visible blood vessels.

Ear sensitivity and visible debris.

All cats have a tendency to develop ear infections and to occasionally have problems with ear mites and similar irritating parasites. A foul odor emanating from the ear is always a key warning sign.

The inner surface of the ear should be clean and smooth in appearance with no visible redness. If the area is inflamed, hot to the touch, and/or black debris is present, the cat's ears should be examined by the vet.

Pale gums and yellow discoloration on the teeth.

A cat's gums should be pink, and the teeth should be clean and white. Any dark or yellow build-up on the teeth is an indication that plaque is present.

Regular dental exams are also critical in detecting any lesions that might indicate the presence of an oral cancer. If found early, such growths can be managed with some success.

Dental care is an extremely important aspect of feline husbandry, with many cat owners actually brushing their cat's teeth using feline toothpaste and brushes available at the veterinary clinic. Never use human products for this purpose on a cat.

While such a regimen may sound absolutely impossible, if started early in a cat's life, the animals are often quite amiable about the whole business. Since it's much more a matter of just getting the paste in the cat's mouth, some owners use their index finger as a "brush".

A dental care kit from a vet typically costs about $7 - $10 / £4.55 - £6.50. It's never too late to start looking after your cat's teeth, and it's certainly worth a try to see how your cat will respond to the process.

Don't worry. You won't lose a finger. If your cat doesn't want any part of dental care, he'll let you know fast enough!

What else to look out for.

There are other factors to consider in monitoring your cat's health on a daily basis.

- Have any growths, masses or bumps evaluated.

- Watch your cat's respiration. It should be from the chest, not the abdomen.

- If the cat goes outside the litter box, immediately have your pet evaluated for kidney and/or bladder infections.

Routine Elements of Health Care

No element of routine health care for your cat is more important than forging a positive relationship with a qualified veterinarian.

While it is true that any "small animal" vet can treat your Birman, I am an advocate of feline-specific practices when they are available.

Offices that are "cats only" tend to be much quieter and have fewer disturbing and threatening scents, which is soothing for patients with a nervous disposition. Birmans are not typically skittish cats, but no pet likes to go to the doctor — any more than we do!

Any time you are considering using a veterinarian, it's a good idea to make an appointment just to interview the doctor. Explain why you are coming in and that you are perfectly willing to pay the usual fee.

Prepare any questions you have in advance. Be on time. Get the information you need, ask for a brief tour of the clinic, and do not overstay your welcome. Vets are busy medical professionals.

You want to get a sense of the vet's personality and the demeanor of the staff as well as the environment and condition of the clinic itself. Only if you are satisfied with what you see and hear should you make a second appointment to take your cat in.

Even at this point in time, however, don't consider the relationship a "done deal". Observe how the vet and the staff interact with your cat, and how your pet reacts to them. This is not just a matter of you getting along with the vet, but of your cat being as comfortable as possible under the circumstances.

Spaying and Neutering

When you adopt a pet quality Birman from a breeder you will be required to agree to have your pet spayed or neutered before six months of age.

If you do not already have a veterinarian, this will be your first opportunity to get your pet established with a health care professional, so you will want to make careful decision in regard to these procedures.

Prices for spaying and neutering vary by clinic, and there are low cost options available for as little as $50 / £32.50, but this may not be the time to think about economy. Take the time to find a vet with whom you plan to work over the course of your cat's life.

It is a tremendous benefit to your cat's long-term well-being for all of its records to be in one place, and for one health care professional to have followed the cat's development through life. If you need a recommendation for a qualified vet, ask your breeder.

Vaccinations

Vaccinations have long been considered a standard aspect of preventive care for small companion animals, but the practice of administering these injections has not been without controversy in recent years. The primary concern is for the potential of tumors developing at the site of the injection.

If you have concerns about the wisdom of vaccinating your Birman you should discuss this matter with both the breeder and your veterinarian.

By the time you take possession of the kitten, it will undoubtedly have received the first round of shots, so you will have to decide if you wish to finish the course of injections or not.

The recommended course of inoculations includes the following vaccines:

Distemper Combo

This injection is administered at six weeks of age with recommended boosters every 3-4 weeks until the cat is 16 weeks old. A second booster will then be given at one year, with subsequent shots every three years for the remainder of your pet's life.

The standard injection is formulated to provide protection for panleukopenia (FPV or feline infectious enteritis), rhinotracheitis (FVR, an upper respiratory / pulmonary infection), and calicivirus (which causes respiratory infections).

There are variations of the vaccine that also provide protection against Chlamydophilia, which causes conjunctivitis.

Feline Leukemia

At 2 months of age the injection for feline leukemia is administered, with a booster to be given 3-4 weeks later. At one year of age, boosters are then given annually for life.

Feline leukemia is an extremely infectious disease that requires only a nose tap for transmission to occur between animals. If your pet is at any risk of coming into contact with cats that live outdoors, this vaccination is extremely important.

Rabies

Often owners do not have a choice about the administration of the rabies vaccine as it is mandated by local law. Proof of compliance is often required as well. Rabies vaccinations are priced at approximately $40 / £26.

Genetic Conditions

As a breed, Birmans are remarkably free of potential genetic diseases. Truthfully, the only conditions of this sort seen with the breed are hypertrophic cardiomyopathy and polycystic kidney disease.

Certainly, overall health should be among the topics you discuss with your breeder while negotiating an adoption.

Hypertrophic Cardiomyopathy

Hypertrophic cardiomyopathy (HCM) thickens the heart muscle causing fluid to accumulate in the lungs and blood clots to form. It can only be confirmed with an echocardiogram.

There is no cure for this condition, which ultimately causes the cat to die of heart failure. Do not believe any breeder that makes the claim that their line is totally free of HCM.

There is no way to guarantee that this genetic fault is not passed on, since, in truth, it can affect a cat of any breed. Most breeders are willing to discuss HCM openly, and to admit if it has been an issue among their cats.

Hip Dysplasia

A defect in the hip socket causes the condition known as hip dysplasia. A cat affected by this problem will move slowly and show a marked reluctance to jump or climb.

The condition presents with a range of severities from mild and annoying to painful and debilitating. Again, there is no way to guarantee that the defect will not show up in any breed of cat.

Maintaining a normal, healthy body weight is a critical component of managing hip dysplasia over a cat's lifetime. Medication may be required for pain control, and at times corrective surgery is indicated.

Polycystic Kidney Disease (PKD)

Polycystic Kidney Disease (PKD) presents at birth with cysts in the kidneys. As the cat ages, the masses grow until they cause the kidneys to fail. PKD becomes detectable in the first 10 years of life; sometimes by the time the animal is 3 years old.

Potential symptoms can include poor appetite and weight loss, extreme thirst and excessive urination, and deterioration of the coat. The cat's gums will be pale from dehydration and it will have bad breath and often ulcers in the mouth. X-rays will show enlargement of the kidneys.

With special diets, the regular administration of subcutaneous fluids, hormone therapy, and antacids, PKD can be managed, but it cannot be cured. The prognosis varies by individual from months to years.

Administering Medications

If you have already had cats in your life, you may have started chuckling just reading the header "administering medications".

Like any sub-culture, "cat people" have their own language. If told by another cat person, "I had to give my cat medicine," the response will likely be the rueful question, "The pink stuff?"

That's a reference to a typical antibiotic given to cats for a number of health problems. It is bright pink and administered with an eyedropper. To say that most cats do not like the "pink stuff," is something of a misnomer.

What cats don't like is being physically restrained while their mouths are pried open and an unwanted liquid is squirted down their throats. Think about that for a minute and you might realize you wouldn't like it either.

There have been great advances in methods of delivery for veterinary medications. When I had a cat suffering from high blood pressure, her medication was a topical cream applied to the inside of the earflap for absorption.

Some medications come as powders that can be hidden effectively in wet food, or even as flavored chews that are sufficiently tasty to cats to be seen as "treats". It isn't always a matter now of holding down an angry, squirming cat and trying to get your pet to swallow liquid or a pill.

When pills and liquids are necessary, I won't lie to you. It can be "game on," with the cat holding a distinct advantage. Never underestimate the level of a cat's determination *not* to do something.

Don't think for a minute that you can hide a pill in a cat's food! Your pet will eat the food and you'll find the pill in pristine condition in the bottom of the bowl.

If you have to give your cat a pill, I recommend a direct, sure and fast approach. Gently take hold of the cat's head from above. Use the index finger of your free hand to open the cat's mouth.

Put the pill as far back in the throat as you can. Gently hold the cat's mouth closed and try stroking your pet's throat to encourage swallowing. Vets have devices called pill "guns" that help to position the pill in the back of the mouth, but I've never been very good with them.

My theory is that the less fuss you make about it all, and the less chance you give the cat to run the show, the more successful you will be. Many people recommend wrapping your pet in a towel first, but I think that just sends the message, "We're getting ready to do something you won't like".

I have found that the same method works well with liquid medication, but I do not like to use the droppers that come with these preparations. I ask for an empty syringe with a mark to indicate dosage.

With the syringe, you benefit from a little more forceful "squirting" of the liquid that further encourages the cat to swallow. If the medicine in question is indeed the "pink stuff," expect your cat to have a little pink fur for a few days (and if I were you, I wouldn't wear white while dispensing the meds).

For any other kind of medications that might have to be administered in the home setting, rely on your vet's advice and ask for a demonstration. I have even given my pets subcutaneous fluid IVs at home. With proper instruction, any home treatment is possible.

Chapter 6 – Pet Insurance and Planning Ahead

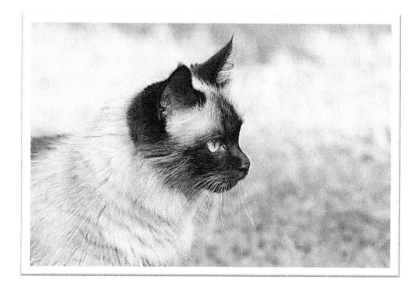

Pet insurance is a relatively new option and one about which owners have many questions. Advances in health care procedures for companion animals have substantially improved the lives of our beloved cats and dogs and extended their life expectancy in fantastic ways, but few if any of these procedures are inexpensive.

Is pet insurance worth the expense? Just as is the case with health insurance for humans, you must understand the reasoning behind paying for a policy. Insurance is intended to help address unexpected large expenses that would represent a serious financial strain if paid out of pocket.

In survey results, significant numbers of pet owners admit they would spend any amount of money to save their pet's life. I have, on more than one occasion, gone into debt to pay for medical treatment for one of my cats.

Thankfully, I have not been put in a position to make an end-of-life decision for one of my pets based on financial hardship, but countless pet owners are put in this horrible position every day.

As companies offering health insurance have grown in number and sophistication, it is now possible to customize policies to select deductible level and copay options (termed "agreed excess levels" in the UK) to arrive at premiums that both protect your pet and fit into your budget.

Having an insurance policy will also broaden your options for treatment should your pet require the services of a specialist. In my case, one of my pets needed radiation treatment for an oral cancer. I borrowed the money, and spent the next four years paying his bills.

Do understand, however, that pet insurance reimbursement works a little differently than the regularly accepted human model:

- You pay the vet directly.

- You are responsible for filing the claim.

- You receive the reimbursement directly.

The reimbursement will include eligible expenses minus the level of your deductible and copy according to the set limits of the policy.

A comprehensive insurance policy for a cat including coverage for accidents, illnesses, and some hereditary conditions with an option for chronic condition coverage can be purchased for $15 - $25 / £9.75 - £16.25 per month depending on the deductible chosen.

Typically such policy caries up to $14,000 / £9,100 a year in benefits and is renewable on an annual basis.

Ask plenty of questions to determine the best company and plan for your needs:

- Can you go to your regular vet, or do you have to go to a vet assigned by the pet insurance company?

- What does the insurance plan cover? Does it cover annual exams? Surgeries? Emergency illness and injury?

- Does coverage begin immediately?

- Are pre–existing conditions covered? In addition, if your cat develops a health issue and you later have to renew the policy, is that condition covered when you renew your policy?

- Is medication covered?

- Do you have to have pre–authorization before your pet receives treatment? What happens if your cat has the treatment without pre–authorization?

- Does the insurance policy cover dental issues and chronic health problems?

- Is there a lifetime maximum benefit amount? If so, how much is that amount? A benefit plan with a lifetime maximum of only a few hundred dollars surely will not suffice!

- Is there an amount that you have to pay before the insurance pays out?

Take the time to research your pet insurance options. Compare the different plans available, what each covers, and the cost before making the decision on which is best for you and your pet.

Pet insurance may not be the answer for everyone. While it may not be a feasible option for you, consider having a backup plan, just in case your cat requires emergency care or you run into unexpected veterinarian costs.

A simple way to prepare for an emergency is to start a veterinary fund for your Birman. Decide to put a certain amount of money aside each week, each month, or each pay–check to use in the case of an emergency. Think about the potential financial costs of veterinary care and plan for how you will pay for it now instead of waiting until something happens.

Companies in the United States offering pet insurance include:

Healthy Paws
HealthyPawsPetInsurance.com

PetPlan
GoPetPlan.com

Embrace
EmbracePetInsurance.com

Trupanion
Trupanion.com

Pets Best
PetsBest.com

Pet Premium
Enroll.PetPremium.com

The ASPCA
ASPCAPetInsurance.com

PetInsurance
PetInsurance.com

Pet First
PetFirst.com

24PetWatch
24PetWatch.com

Pet insurance companies in the United Kingdom include:

DirectLine
Directline.com/pet-insurance

VetsMediCover
Vetsmedicover.co.uk

PetPlan
Petplan.co.uk

Churchill
Churchill.com/pet-insurance

Animal Friends
Animalfriends.org.uk

Healthy Pets
Healthy-pets.co.uk

For a comprehensive comparison of policies see:
Money.co.uk/pet-insurance.htm

Please note that all companies and links were active at the time of publication in early 2014, but like all Internet content are subject to change. Since pet insurance is growing rapidly in popularity, use the search engine of your choice to look for additional coverage options. Note that the vast majority of sites allow visitors to obtain an estimate price quote online.

Planning for the Unexpected

If something happens to you, you want to know that your cat and any other pets will be properly cared for and loved. Some cell phones allow you to input an ICE (In Case of Emergency) number with notes. If your cell phone has such an option, use it. If it does not, write the following information on a piece of a paper and put it in your wallet with your driver's license:

- The names of each of your pets, including your cat.

- The names and phone numbers of family members or friends who have agreed to temporarily care for your pets in an emergency.

- The name and phone number of your veterinarian.

Be sure to also talk with your neighbors, letting them know how many pets you have and the type of pets. That way, if something happens to you, they can alert the authorities, ensuring your pets do not linger for days before they are found.

If you fail to do that and something happens to you, someone will find your cat and any other pets and will need to know what to do to ensure that they are cared for. It is a good idea in the case of an emergency, to ask several friends or family members to be responsible for taking care of your pets should something happen to you.

Prepare instructions for the intended guardians, providing amended instructions as necessary. Also, be sure to provide each individual with a key to your home (remember to inform your home insurance company so that this does not affect your coverage). Instructions should include:

- The name and phone numbers of each individual who agreed to take care of your cat and other pets.

- Your pet's diet and feeding schedule.

- The name and phone number of your veterinarian.

- Any health problems and medications your cat may take on a daily basis, including dosage instructions, instructions on how to give the medicine, and where the medicine is kept.

Put as much information as necessary to ensure the guardians can provide the same level of care to which your cat is accustomed.

Chapter 7 – To Breed or Not To Breed

Over the years, I have been involved with the breeding of cats. I loved and enjoyed the experience, but I urge you to really think before taking that step. I have seen far too many cases of well-intentioned, enthusiastic people who start a cattery only to experience failure because they weren't truly prepared.

In these cases, the ones who suffer the most are the cats. That is the thing we all want to avoid, and what is always the most heartbreaking for the would-be cat breeder. There's a terrific amount of guilt in the aftermath of a failed breeding operation.

No matter how rewarding you think the project might be, and I assure you can be, it's important that you consider the implications of running a cattery for both you and your family. For this reason, there are a number of things I'd like to suggest that you contemplate fully.

The decision to become a breeder of Birman cats or any other type of cat is one of those choices that may well *sound* better in theory than it plays out to be in reality. If you are considering becoming a breeder, understand from the beginning that you are not contemplating a mere hobby.

Dedicated breeders live and breathe the world of their cats. They share their lives with their cats, or, to put a finer point on it, order their lives according to the needs of their cats.

Also, do not think that becoming a cat breeder is a way to make money. If you have just paid a handsome price for a purebred Birman you may well snort at this assertion in disbelief. Yes, purebred kittens command high prices, but ask any breeder what happens to that money as soon as it comes into their hands.

Their answer will be a firm assurance that the amount goes right back out the door — to pay for vet bills, or cat food, or an addition on the house for the cats or any one of a hundred other cattery related expenses. Breeders who are honest will admit that in a good year, they break even.

There is only one reason to become involved in breeding cats — *love of the breed.*

Questions to Ask Yourself

If you are thinking about becoming a breeder, you need to immerse yourself in the culture of the cat fancy. Attend cat shows and make contact with existing breeders.

When you understand more about cat shows, you'll know that the event itself is not the place to try to have a discussion with a breeder. Instead, use these venues to collect business cards and to see examples of the breed in which you're interested.

Look for local Birman clubs to join, and find online discussion forums to learn more from working breeders. Let me interject a word about forum etiquette. Never just jump into discussions as a "newbie". Spend a few weeks learning the culture of the forum before you post. It is far too easy to give offense without realizing what you are doing.

There are numerous questions you must pose to yourself. The contacts you make and the discussions you have with people knowledgeable about Birmans and the operation of a cattery will guide you in forming your answers. Be honest with yourself! This is just a short list of things to consider:

- Do you have the time, including nights, weekends, holidays, to devote to the needs of your animals?

- Are you willing to allow your schedule to be dominated — often at a moment's notice — by your cats?

- Are you prepared for the heartache when kittens don't live?

- Are you prepared to see the kittens you have raised go to new homes? No matter how well you screen the adoptive parents or how much money you charge, that is still going to be a painful good-bye.

- Can you cover the initial financial outlay to not only make physical changes to your home, but also to acquire either a high quality queen or a breeding pair?

- Do you live in a setting that is even appropriate for this kind of endeavor? Are there zoning considerations? Homeowners association regulations? Tax implications?

Above all, outline Plan B. Of course you want to go into your new venture with optimism and enthusiasm, but temper that with a healthy dose of realism.

Know what you will do if it all goes wrong. You are bringing living creatures into your care. If you can't sustain the operation of your cattery, what will happen to them?

Memberships

You will gain more information and education from seeking out and joining breed clubs and professional breeder organizations. While there may not be a specific group for every breed, start with a major parent organization like The International Cat Association.

Even if the breed in which you are interested does not have a breeder's association per se, membership in major governing groups will help you to make contact with established breeders and potentially develop a mentoring relationship.

In the United States you can find further information from the National Birman Fanciers at
www.nationalbirmanfanciers.com

while in the United Kingdom you can begin with
The Birman Cat Club at
www.birmancatclub.co.uk

Details of other clubs around the world can be found at
www.birmanbreeder.com

Compiling Estimated Costs

It is almost impossible to know all the costs that might be involved for any one person in setting up a cattery. My best advice to you is to imagine every possible expense and plan for it. Some of the more obvious items on this list should be:

Reference Materials

You are going to need to know everything there is to know about the Birman breed and its genetics. You will need reference materials including subscriptions to feline publications.

Foundation Animals

If you cannot afford a breeding pair, you will at least need a quality queen or stud. You will then need to factor in the cost of pairing your animal with a suitable mate from another cattery.

Veterinary Care

This is obviously a major routine expense for normal health care, but factor in infant and maternal services. Discuss the potential for problem pregnancies with your vet and find out in advance what emergency procedures like C-sections might cost.

You will also have to pay for repeat testing for your queen or stud if they are to go "visit" another cattery. At minimum you will have to produce the results of a recent FELV/FIV test each time.

Equipment, Furniture, Toys

In looking at these expenses, make a complete sub-list and then multiply the costs for everything including, but not limited to: cages, travel crates, play pens, climbing trees, beds and toys.

You will likely be creating an entire cat "room," so think about any kind of furniture you will need or any physical changes to the room that may be required to prevent escapes and enhance its security.

Construction Costs

If you have to add a room on to your house, work with a contractor well in advance of ever purchasing your breeding stock. Everything must be in place before you acquire your cats. If construction costs are prohibitive, this factor alone could derail your plans.

Insurance Considerations

It is impossible to predict the insurance considerations for every individual circumstance. If you are planning to start a cattery, however, a visit with your insurance agent is a must.

You may have to increase your coverage limits or add policy amendments or "riders" to cover additional equipment or square footage and to allow for visitors to your premises.

It is possible that you will also require both liability and indemnity insurance. Work with your agent to determine the appropriate level of coverage for your circumstances and to gain an estimate of the additional premium costs.

Emergency Reserve

It's considered "best practice" to have a 3-6 month operating reserve in cash. This is especially crucial if you are put in a position to shut down your operation since you will still have to feed and care for your animals during the time you are placing them in new homes.

Do not proceed without this emergency reserve in place. It's simply not fair to the innocent animals which will be depending on you completely for their well-being.

Going Forward

I've tried to be constructive in laying out some of the challenges and tribulations that will lie ahead of you as I feel it is important to contemplate and reflect on these before taking that big step.

I have seen too many cases of people with the best of intention and enthusiasm start an enterprise only for it to fail due to lack of preparation and thought with the only ones suffering as a result being their cats.

No matter how rewarding you think it might be, it is important that you consider the implications on your lifestyle and that of your family.

If my comments and observations haven't deterred you, then I applaud and welcome you to a most wonderful and challenging pastime which provides so much love and joy. The thrill and sense of achievement you will get from breeding your own Birman Cat is one that I know you will cherish and treasure in the years to come.

Chapter 8 – Showing Birman Cats

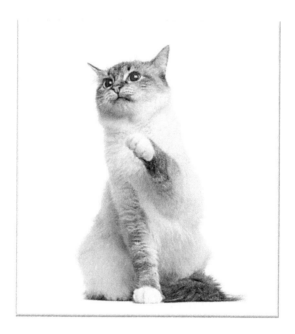

People who breed Birman cats do so in part to showcase the excellence of their bloodlines, so in this regard, participating in showing is an aspect of their business operations. An impressive collection of awards lends a high degree of prestige to any cattery.

At the same time, however, these people are dedicated proponents of the breeds they cultivate. Remember, however, that if you have purchased a Birman from a breeder, you have probably bought a "pet quality" animal. Show quality exemplars of the breed are easily twice the cost.

If you have a show quality cat, there is nothing to keep you from joining the show circuit. The Birman Breed, with its easy going, adaptable personality and calm demeanor, does better than many breeds with the whole process.

This must be, however, something of a "joint" decision. You have to decide showing is something you want to do, and then you must judge your pet's suitability to be shown. I am a firm believer that no animal should be made absolutely miserable just to be on a quest for a ribbon.

My best advice to you is to attend cat shows for the purpose of watching and learning. I'm about to run down the basics for you, but you have to experience a show first hand to get even the vaguest sense of the world you're thinking about entering.

The World of the Cat Show

I'm getting ready to give you a lot of information about cat shows, but I want you to hear one thing loudly and clearly from the beginning. When you go to a cat show DO NOT TOUCH THE CATS.

Don't Touch

Yes, you will be in the presence of cats that are physically beautiful and the urge will be overwhelming. Beyond the fact that it's bad manners, you represent a danger to those cats — or more specifically whatever is living on your hands represents a danger.

We walk around with bacteria and viruses on our hands at all times. As already noted, many feline diseases are so contagious all the animals have to do is tap noses to be infected. They don't need our help spreading germs all over their bodies petting them.

And what is the first thing a cat does after a good petting? Licks every hair to get the human scent off. I'm not being facetious. Cats prefer to smell like cats. They like the petting just fine, but they will still groom to make themselves smell the way they think they should.

If you have germs all over your hands, and the cat then licks its fur, the potential for illness is enormous. This is the reason for the "don't touch" rule.

Being invited to touch a cat at a cat show is a huge compliment, one usually extended along with a jar of hand sanitizer. Don't even blink. Use the sanitizer. Do it for the cat.

Don't Help

The second rule after don't touch is don't help. The cry of "loose cat" is heard fairly often in these venues. When a cat makes a break for it, the appropriate thing to do is freeze and be quiet.

Under no circumstances should you join the chase. You'll just frighten the escapee more. If you see the cat, get the attention of the owner and quietly signal where the cat is located.

Get Out of the Way

One thing you do want to do at a cat show is get out of the way. Often you'll hear a rushing exhibitor yell, "Right of way!" That's your cue to yield!

For that matter, don't be surprised if an exhibitor stops talking with you mid-sentence and goes dashing off. When exhibitors are called to the ring, they have only a limited amount of time to get there or be disqualified.

Do not be put off or offended by these instances. Cat shows can be very hectic and chaotic events. Don't contribute to the chaos.

Look and Listen

Remember that you are there to learn. Don't just look at the cats. Observe what's going on. Write down things you want to investigate or questions you want to ask.

Especially when you're near the ring where the judging is going on, be quiet and listen. You'll learn a great deal from the comments the judges make in the ring, and you certainly do not want to distract the exhibitors or the cats.

Cat Show Basics

While this may be the most obvious of statements, a cat show is not a dog show. There are definite differences in how the two kinds of events are run.

For starters, cats are kept secured at all times. Show cats stay in their cages, which are often quite elaborately decorated to call attention to both the animal and the cattery.

This fact lends a festive air to the whole exhibit hall, but the cage rule is strictly a matter of security. The idea is to avoid the "loose cat" situation, although, as we've discussed, that still happens all too often.

A point that is difficult for newbies to grasp is that in terms of movement, cat shows are very, very slow. However, when something is happening, they turn hectic in a heartbeat — like the regular mad dashes to the show ring.

Cat shows include a class for household pets; dog shows do not. The pet category is responsible for attracting many young people to the cat fancy and is a highly popular part of any show.

Judges evaluate all animals by breed standards formalized by the various agencies responsible for hosting and governing shows. Most of these standards follow or closely resemble the one established by The International Cat Association, which I provide for you later in this chapter.

The various governing bodies for cat shows include:

- The International Cat Association

- Fédération Internationale Féline

- World Cat Federation

- Cat Fanciers Association

- Feline Federation Europe

- Australia Cat Federation

- American Association of Cat Enthusiasts

- American Cat Fanciers Association

Is Showing Right for You and Your Cat?

Before you make the decision to show the Birman, or any other breed for that matter, you have a lot of research to do — on the breed in general, on your cat specifically, on the cat fancy, and on cat shows.

You do not have to participate in the world of the cat fancy to share your life with a beautiful pedigree animal, nor do you have to raise pure bred cats to enjoy their company.

Breeding and showing are pastimes and avocations that should have no other goals but furthering the development of the breed and supporting the welfare of the cats.

Only move forward with showing your cat if you are positive it is the right move for you, but especially, if it is the right move for your cat. If your pet is going to be miserable at a cat show, don't do it. No ribbon is worth that.

TICA Birman Cat Show Standard

Head Total: 35

Shape	5
Ears	5
Eyes	5
Chin	5
Muzzle	5
Nose	5
Profile	5

Body Total: 25

Torso	5
Legs	5
Feet	5
Boning	5
Musculature	5

Coat/Color/Pattern Total: 30

Length	5
Texture	5

Pattern	10
Color	10
Other Total: 10	
Balance	5
Condition	5

CATEGORIES: Pointed

DIVISION: Solid Point/White, Tortie Point/White, Tabby Point/White and Silver and/or Smoke Point /White, gloved pattern only.

COLORS: All

PERMISSIBLE OUTCROSSES: None

HEAD:

Shape: The head is strong, broad, and rounded from frontal view; slightly longer than wide in profile. Cheeks are full.

Ears: The ears are almost as wide at the base as they are tall. They should be open at the base, have a slightly rounded tip, and be medium in size, and placed moderately far apart with furnishings.

Eyes: The eyes are medium to large, moderately rounded, and set fairly wide apart. They are blue in color, the deeper the better.

Chin: The chin has good depth, forming a perpendicular line with upper lip.

Muzzle: The muzzle has medium length, with enough width to prevent a pinched look

Nose: The nose is medium in length and is roman in shape with nostrils set low.

Profile: The forehead is sloped back with a slight transverse flat spot in the middle of the forehead just above the eye ridge. There is a change of direction between the forehead and the roman nose.

BODY:

Torso: The Birman is a full-bodied, medium long, sturdy cat with a level back. The overall size is medium to large. The neck is strong and well-muscled, thicker on breeding males. In all respects, males are generally larger than females.

Legs: The legs are medium in length, heavily boned, well-muscled, and in good proportion to the body.

Feet: The feet are large, rounded, and firm.

Tail: The tail is full and in good proportion to the body.

Musculature: Firm and strong.

COAT:

Length: Semi-long to long.

Texture: Silky with no undercoat.

Miscellaneous: Heavy ruff is desirable, especially in males. Fur can be slightly curly on the stomach. Seasonal changes should be considered when judging coat length.

Pattern: Gloves and Laces: All Birmans should have white feet. Front paws have white gloves, preferably ending in an even line across paws at third joint (where toes meet paws). The back paws have white gloves covering the front of each paw, extending up the back of the legs ending in a point approximately half way up the hock ("laces"). Evenly matched gloves and laces give a more balanced look, but variations are allowed. The paw pads may be all pink or spotted with color the same as the points. Gloves and Laces are weighted equally in evaluation. Although the Gloves and Laces are important aspects of the Birman, they are secondary to conformation.

Color: Birmans are pointed in all colors. Coat color and point color are weighted equally in evaluation.

OTHER:

Balance: The Birman is a well-balanced cat, not extreme in any way.

Condition: The Birman should be in top health condition, with a clean, well-groomed coat and body.

GENERAL DESCRIPTION: The Sacred Cat of Burma (Birman) is a semi-longhaired pointed cat with white feet. He is imposing in appearance, medium to large in stature, with heavy boning in proportion to size. Females are appreciably smaller than males. The Birman is to be healthy, muscular, and in good balance. The coat has a tendency not to mat or tangle. The Birman is accepted in all pointed colors with distinctive white gloves and laces.

ALLOWANCES: Age may produce shading or darkening of the coat color, which is acceptable. Freckling on the lip and/or ear areas in the Red Factor points is allowed. Paw pads spotted with color is allowed. Lockets.

PENALIZE: Areas of white extending above the level of the dew pad on the rear of the front leg, lack of one or both laces, free spots of point color in gloves or laces (excluding the paw pads).

WITHHOLD ALL AWARDS (WW): Lack of any white on any foot, and free areas of white in the mask, ears, or tail.

Temperament must be unchallenging; any sign of definite challenge shall disqualify. The cat may exhibit fear, seek to flee, or generally complain aloud but may not threaten to harm. In accordance with Show Rules, ARTICLE SIXTEEN, the following shall be considered mandatory disqualifications: a cat that bites (216.9), a cat showing evidence of intent to deceive (216.10), adult whole male cats not having two descended testicles (216.11), cats with all or part of the tail missing , except as authorized by a Board approved standard (216.12.1), cats with more than five toes on each front foot and four toes on each back foot, unless proved the result of an injury or as authorized by a Board approved standard (216.12.2), visible or invisible tail faults if Board approved standard requires disqualification (216.12.4), crossed eyes if Board approved standard requires disqualification (216.12.5), total blindness (216.12.6), markedly smaller size, not in keeping with the breed (216.12.9), and depression of the sternum or unusually small diameter of the rib cage itself (216.12.11.1). See Show Rules, ARTICLE SIXTEEN for more comprehensive rules governing penalties and disqualifications.

Revised 05/01/09 Birman Standard, 05/01/2009

Chapter 9 – Birman Cats Care Sheet

Price $500 - $600 / £298 - £357

Physical Characteristics

Size: Medium to large cats.

Build: Strong

Weight: 8 - 12 lbs. / 3.62 - 5.44 kg

Coat: Silky, semi-longhaired, no undercoat.

Color: Light bodies with color points and white feet.

Lifespan: 12-16 years

Grooming

Birmans are semi-longhaired cats. Because they do not have an undercoat, they are not prone to matting. Weekly combing and the occasional bath is all that will be required to keep your cat's coat in good condition.

Personality

Birmans are calm, quiet, and docile cats with an active and curious nature. They are definitely people cats, and while not all are lap cats, Birmans do like to be with their people and will get lonely if left by themselves too long. Overall, these are very sweet and companionable cats.

Food and Water for Adults

Dry Food – Give a quarter to half a cup per day or 2 to 4 ounces / 56.7 to 113 grams.

Wet food – Give approximately 5.5 ounces / 156 grams once to twice daily.

Provide a constant source of clean fresh water.

Litter Box

Texture of litter and type of box to the cat's preference, scooped daily and changed out completely 1-2 times per week.

Health Care

Initial spaying or neutering with regular program of vaccinations in consultation with a qualified veterinarian. General preventive health care including dental. A hardy breed but both hypertrophic cardiomyopathy and hip dysplasia are possible.

Chapter 10 – Closing Thoughts

From the moment I saw Pumpkin, my friend Julie's Birman cat, gazing down at me from the top of the refrigerator, I have been a huge fan of this breed.

I have fond memories of grading exam books in my friend's apartment, spreading them out on the carpet with Pumpkin helpfully holding them in place for us.

She was always present when we studied or worked — with us, but never in the way, occasionally batting a catnip mouse into the middle of things to keep us from taking ourselves too seriously.

I have no doubt that Julie acknowledged the help of "P.C. Berman" in the front matter of her thesis with real gratitude for the sweet animal's companionship and gentle affection.

If the origin myth for the breed is to be believed, the Birman's pure white paws are a symbol of their loyalty and devotion to their humans, traits I have witnessed firsthand.

As a confirmed "crazy cat lady," I have a deep set love for all cats. I like their way of being in the world, and find nothing quite so comforting as a cat's inscrutable and seeming wise gaze.

Birmans are among my favorite of all the longhaired breeds. They are soft and silky, but require only weekly combing to stay in good condition. There is very little shedding, even seasonally.

I am also attracted to the length of their lifespan of 12-16 years and their remarkably hardy constitutions. For prospective owners, I would urge that you carefully evaluate how much time you spend at home.

Birmans will get lonely if left by themselves excessively, but this is easily mitigated by keeping two cats, or even a cat and a dog. This breed does quite well with other companion animals and they are a good fit for families with responsible and well behaved children.

This is not, however, a breed that should have even partial access to the outdoors. Beyond the fact that all longhaired cats should be kept inside for considerations of grooming, Birmans are too docile for outside circumstances.

If, after considering all these factors, you think that a Birman is right for you, be prepared to fall in love. All it takes is meeting those sapphire blue eyes once, and you'll be hooked — I know I was.

Chapter 11 – Relevant Websites

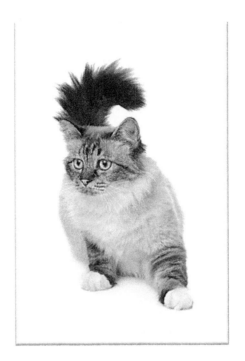

The Cat Fanciers Association, Inc.
www.cfainc.org

The International Cat Association
www.tica.org

Birman Cat Club of Canberra
www.actbirmanclub.com.au

Birman Cat Club of New Zealand
www.birmancatclub.co.nz

The Birman Cat Club ~ UK
www.birmancatclub.co.uk

National Birman Fanciers (CFA)
www.nationalbirmanfanciers.com

North American Birman Fanciers
www.birman.org

Sacred Cat of Burma Fanciers (CFA)
www.scbf.com

Birman Welfare and Rescue
www.birmanrescue.co.uk

Shopping

SOMETHING FOR EVERYONE & THEIR CAT

www.PamperedCatShop.com

www.PamperedCatShop.co.uk

Chapter 12 – Frequently Asked Questions

W hile I recommend that you read the entire text to get a good sense of life with a Birman, for those of you who like to get a "quick start" on a subject, these are some of the most frequently asked questions I encounter about this breed.

What should I look for in selecting a Birman kitten?

Generally kittens that are offered for adoption are at least 12 weeks of age. They should be happy and interested, with only a little initial shyness. There should be no discharge from the eyes and ears, and the ears should be clean with no odor.

Healthy kittens have soft, shiny fur that is thick and intact with no thin or bald spots. The body should feel solid and healthy, not bony. Good hydration should be evident in the gums, which should be pink and moist.

What's the best way to find a good breeder?

One of the best ways to get in touch with high-quality breeders is to attend cat shows. Catteries exhibit their finest animals at these venues and, while you cannot adopt on the spot, you can collect business cards.

Do Birmans need any kind of special diet?

Any cat may need a special diet to help in the management of a health condition, but most cats, including Birmans, thrive on a balanced and varied diet of high-quality wet and dry foods.

How much grooming is required for a Birman cat?

On a weekly basis, 5-15 minutes of combing and brushing should keep a Birman's coat in excellent condition. These cats do not have an undercoat, so tangling and matting is not an issue as it is in other longhaired breeds like the Persian.

What equipment is needed for grooming?

The best implement for the Birman coat is a metal comb with alternating short and long teeth.

At what age should I begin to groom my Birman?

The sooner a cat becomes accustomed to daily grooming, the better. If you buy your Birman from a reputable breeder, the kitten should already be used to being combed. Replicate the existing routine as closely as possible.

Will my Birman shed more seasonally?

Longhaired cats shed more in the summer months. Starting in the spring, you'll see an increased need for combing, perhaps daily, to stay ahead of the shedding and to prevent mats and tangles.

Is there any difference in temperament and adaptability in a male or female Birman?

The gender question really isn't a valid concern. All cats are individuals with unique personalities. Cats, like people, develop in response to their life experiences.

I've had cats of many breeds of both genders. I've rarely found gender to be an indicator of personality, and it is certainly not an issue with Birmans. All are well mannered, sweet and agreeable.

Is there a problem with a male Birman spraying?

I have never had an issue with male cats of any breed spraying, regardless of their intact or altered status. The behavior is even less likely in neutered males.

The neutering surgery is performed before six months of age. At that stage, the cats are just too young to start spraying.

Female cats can spray as well, although they do so only rarely. I think it's fair to say that well cared for, happy, healthy cats don't display problem behavior of any kind, including spraying.

The spraying stereotype is, in my opinion, unfairly applied to male cats. If it does happen, it likely indicates a cat that is either unhappy or physically ill.

Appendix 1 – Birman Cat Breeders List

A worldwide list can be found at
www.birmanbreeder.com/site.htm

United States

Arkansas

Birquest
www.birquest.com

California

Kissyfurs
www.kissyfursbirmans.com

Iowa

Kanza Katz
www.kanzakatz.bravehost.com

Kentucky

ForHim
www.forhimbirmans.com

Minnesota

Kats Kits
www.katskits.com

Missouri

Templkatz
www.templkatz.com

New Jersey

Pixydust
www.pixydustbirmans.com

Pennsylvania

LilRascals
www.lilrascal.com

Texas

BumbleBe
www.bumblebebirmans.com

Virginia

Oshkosh
www.oshkoshbirmans.bravehost.com

United Kingdom

Arezza Birmans – Norwich, Norfolk
Tracy Adams
Adamst@arezzacats.fsnet.co.uk
http://arezzabirmans.webs.com

Tisanti Birmans – South Wales
Matthew Allen
pallenspain10@yahoo.co.uk
www.tisanticattery.com

Nicadaemus Birmans - Wiltshire
Nicola Bailey
nicolasbailey@btopenworld.com
www.nicadaemus.com

Elmarlay Birmans - Kingswinford
Wayne Baxter
baxtella@yahoo.co.uk
www.thecatsofelmarlay.co.uk

Munkchip Birmans – Bristol
Sandra Bennett & Emma Baker
munkchipbirmans@yahoo.co.uk
www.munkchipbirmans.webs.com

Lizzara Birmans - Lockerbie, Scotland
Ginny Black
ginny@lizzara.com
www.facebook.com/pages/Lizzara-Birmans-Siberians-
Norwegian-Forest-Cats/382761021739921

Bydezyne Birmans – Yorkshire
Heather Collings
bydezyne@hotmail.com
www.bydezyne.co.uk/bydezyne_birmans.htm

Jenicol Birmans - Sanderstead, Surrey
M Griffiths
jenicol@fsmail.net
www.jenicolbirmans.webs.com

Churston Birmans - Rochford, Essex
Gale & David Griggs
churstonuk@aol.com
www.churstonbirmans.co.uk

Mentobe Birmans - Tividale
Mark & Susie Harris
mentobe.birmans@blueyonder.co.uk
www.mentobecats.weebly.com

Yokota Birmans - Dunstable, Bedfordshire
Amanda Lachlan
amanda@yokota-cats.co.uk
www.yokota-cats.co.uk

Ladypaws Birmans - Mansfield
Ann Methven
ann@ladypaws.co.uk
www.diannesladypawsbirmans.com

Lavalna Birman and Maine Coons
Natalie Hough
nataliehough1@hotmail.co.uk
www.lavalna.webs.com

Jandouglen Birmans
Ann V.C. Mott
ann.mott@freeuk.com
www.ann.mott.freeuk.com

LongWells Birmans – (FKA Aylpurrtona Birmans
Lydney, Gloucestershire
Colin & Stella Newman
stellatump@aol.com
www.longwells-birmans.co.uk

Siolu Birmans - Salisbury, Wiltshire
Jeni Nutley
jenicat@hotmail.co.uk
www.siolubirmans.co.uk

Rozinella Birmans - Thornton Heath, Surrey
Maria Oslavio
rozinella@aol.com
www.freewebs.com/rozinellabirmans

Goldlay Birmans - Buckinghamshire
Marcia Owen
Marcia@goldlay-cats.co.uk
www.goldlay-cats.co.uk

Little Boots Birmans - Rochester
Serena Pearson-Bish
mail@littleboots.co.uk
www.meowhoo.com/Detailed/6940.html

Alvagem Birmans - Bedfordshire
Karen Porteous
Karen.Porteous@Tesco.net

Bostin Birmans - West Midlands
Darren & Stacey Skelding
Skeldings@BostinBirmans.com
www.bostinbirmans.blogspot.com

Shandatal Birmans – Wixford, Warwickshire
Shirley Talboys
satalboys@shandatal.co.uk
www.shandatal.co.uk

Tarkusha Birmans - East Sussex
Geoffrey Tarr
Geoff_Tarr@msn.com
www.tarkusha.bizland.com

Lachmere Birmans - Staffordshire
Angela Walker
lachmere@aol.com
www.lachmerebirmans.webs.com

Bluducati Birmans - Ilfracombe
Mr & Mrs P White
spwhite@bluducati.eclipse.co.uk
www.bluducati-birmans.co.uk

Canada

BoJo Birmans
juliaduguid@bojobirmans.com
Edmonton, Alberta
www.bojobirmans.com

Pussetoe Birmans
Linda Birkmann
Linda@pussetoebirmans.com
Pussetoe
http://pussetoebirmans.com

Skyhaven Birman Cattery
Anastasia Sky
docsky@sympatico.ca
Hamilton, Ontario
http://skyhavenbirmans.com

Chatterie Doux Velours
Doris Guite
info@douxvelours.com
Carleton-sur-Mer, Québec
www.douxvelours.com

Angel Eyes Birmans
Sylvia Foulds
Birmancats@shaw.ca
Edmonton
www.angel-eyes.ca

Appendix 2 – Toxic Plants List

The following is a fairly comprehensive though not exhaustive list but please check with your breeder or veterinarian for dangerous plants and flowers in your area.

Almond (pits)

Aloe Vera

Alocasia

Amaryllis

American Yew

Apple (seeds)

Apple Leaf Croton

Apricot (pits)

Arrowgrass

Asparagus Fern

Autumn Crocus

Avocado (fruit and pit)

Azalea Baby's Breath

Baneberry

Bayonet

Beargrass

Beech

Belladonna

Bird of Paradise

Bittersweet

Black-eyed Susan

Black Locust

Bleeding Heart

Bloodroot

Bluebonnet

Box

Boxwood

Branching Ivy

Buckeyes

Buddhist Pine

Burning Bush

Buttercup Cactus

Candelabra

Caladium

Calla Lily

Castor Bean

Ceriman

Charming Dieffenbachia

Cherry (pits, seeds, leaves)

Cherry Laurel

Chinaberry

Chinese Evergreen

Christmas Rose

Chrysanthemum

Cineria

Clematis

Cordatum

Coriaria

Cornflower

Corn Plant

Cornstalk Plant

Croton

Corydalis

Crocus, Autumn

Crown of Thorns

Cuban Laurel

Cutleaf Philodendron

Cycads

Cyclamen

Daffodil

Daphne

Datura

Deadly Nightshade	Euonymus
Death Camas	Evergreen Ferns
Devil's Ivy	Fiddle-leaf Fig
Delphinium	Florida Beauty
Decentrea	Flax
Dieffenbachia	Four O'Clock
Dracaena Palm	Foxglove
Dragon Tree	Fruit Salad Plant
Dumb Cane	Geranium
Easter Lily	German Ivy
Eggplant	Giant Dumb Cane
Elaine	Glacier Ivy
Elderberry	Golden Chain
Elephant Ear	Gold Dieffenbachia
Emerald Feather	Gold Dust Dracaena
English Ivy	Golden Glow
English Yew	Golden Pothos
Eucalyptus	Gopher Purge

Hahn's Self-Branching Ivy	Jack in the Pulpit
Heartland Philodendron	Janet Craig Dracaena
Hellebore	Japanese Show Lily
Hemlock, Poison	Java Beans
Hemlock, Water	Jessamine
Henbane	Jerusalem Cherry
Holly	Jimson Weed
Horsebeans	Jonquil
Horsebrush	Jungle Trumpets
Hellebore	Kalanchoe
Horse Chestnuts	Lacy Tree Philodendron
Hurricane Plant	Lantana
Hyacinth	Larkspur
Hydrangea	Laurel
Indian Rubber Plant	Lily
Indian Tobacco	Lily Spider
Iris	Lily of the Valley
Iris Ivy	Locoweed

Lupine	Nephytis
Madagascar Dragon Tree	Nightshade Oleander
Marble Queen	Onion
Marigold	Oriental Lily
Marijuana	Peace Lily
Mescal Bean	Peach (pits and leaves)
Mexican Breadfruit	Pencil Cactus
Miniature Croton	Peony
Mistletoe	Periwinkle
Mock Orange	Philodendron
Monkshood	Pimpernel
Moonseed	Plumosa Fern
Morning Glory	Poinciana
Mother-in-Law's Tongue	Poinsettia (low toxicity)
Mountain Laurel	Poison Hemlock
Mushrooms	Poison Ivy
Narcissus	Poison Oak
Needlepoint Ivy	Pokeweed

Poppy	Scotch Broom
Potato	Silver Pothos
Pothos	Skunk Cabbage
Precatory Bean	Snowdrops
Primrose	Snow on the Mountain
Privet, Common	Spotted Dumb Cane
Red Emerald	Staggerweed
Red Princess	Star of Bethlehem
Red-Margined Dracaena	String of Pearls
Rhododendron	Striped Dracaena
Rhubarb	Sweetheart Ivy
Ribbon Plan	Sweetpea
Rosemary Pea	Swiss Cheese plant
Rubber Plant	Tansy Mustard
Saddle Leaf Philodendron	Taro Vine
Sago Palm	Tiger Lily
Satin Pathos	Tobacco
Schefflera	Tomato Plant (green fruit, stem, leaves)

Tree Philodendron	Wild Call
Tropic Snow Dieffenbachia	Western Yew
	Wisteria Yews
Tulip	Yew, American
Tung Tree	Yew, English
Virginia Creeper	Yew, Western
Water Hemlock	Yew, Wisteria
Weeping Fig	

Source: The Cat Fancier's Association,
CFA.org/CatCare/HouseholdHazards/ToxicPlants.aspx

Glossary

A

Ailurophile – One who loves and is actively involved with cats. Also a committed member of the cat fancy.

Ailurophobe – Any person who harbors a dislike of cats or who has a fear of cats. This can be in response to a bad experience, a simple expression of preference, or an actual phobia.

Allergen – The primary allergen in cats is the protein Fel d 1, which is produced by the animal's saliva and sebaceous glands. In people with sensitivity, Fel d 1 triggers a pronounced allergic reaction.

Allergy – An allergy is a pronounced sensitivity to an environmental agent that triggers a cascade of responses in a sensitive person including, but not limited to, sneezing, watering eyes, itching and skin rashes.

Alter – An accepted term indicating that a cat or dog has been neutered or spayed and thus made incapable of reproduction. A similar, colloquial term frequently used with the same meaning is "fixed".

B

Bloodline – In pedigreed cats, the bloodline is the animal's verifiable line of descent. It is used for the purposes of establishing pedigree.

Breed Standard – Feline governing organizations publish established sets of standards outline the points considered necessary for an individual animal to be regarded as a perfect example of any given breed. The standards are used for the purpose of judging at cat shows.

Breed – Any group of cats with a defined set of physical characteristics that are reliably passed on to subsequent generations and that distinguish them from other types of cats is said to be a distinct "breed".

Breeder - A breeder is a person who works with male and female cats of a particular breed, pairing the animals to produce offspring that exhibit exceptionally high quality according to the accepted standards for the type of cat in question.

Breeding - In the sense of an organized promulgation of a breed within the cat fancy, breeding is the process whereby sires and dams are paired with an eye toward the superior quality of their offspring.

Breeding Program – A breeding program is an organized effort to selectively breed superior individuals of any type of cat for the express purpose of producing offspring of exceptional quality.

Breeding Quality – A cat is said to be of breeding quality when it exhibits sufficiently superior traits according to the accepted breed standard to be regarded as suitable for participation in an organized breeding program.

Breed True – When cats of the same breed pass on an identifiable set of physical characteristics from one generation to the next, those traits are said to "breed true". These might include such things as coat color or type, eye color, or physical conformation.

C

Carpal Pads - A cat's carpal pads are found on the animal's front legs at the "wrists". These pads serve to provide additional traction to the animal when walking.

Castrate – Castration is the medical procedure for the removal of a male cat's testicles to render the animal incapable of reproduction.

Caterwaul - A caterwaul is a high-pitched and strident feline vocalization that is discordant and unpleasant.

Cat Fancy – The "cat fancy" is comprised of those individuals actively interested in breeding, showing, and even simply appreciating cats of various breeds and types as well as the registered associations and clubs to which they belong.

Catnip – Catnip is a perennial herb in the mint family. Its scientific name is *Nepeta cataria*. Many cats are strongly attracted to catnip and exhibit mild intoxication upon contact with it. Kittens cannot experience this response, however, until they are at least 6-9 months of age.

Cattery – A cattery is any establishment where cats are housed, usually as part of an organized program of breeding.

Certified Pedigree – Certified pedigrees are issued by feline registering associations and are a validation of an individual animal's genetic authenticity as a prime example of a given breed.

Clowder – Clowder is a collective name indicating a group of cats gathered in one place at one time.

Coat – Coat is the accepted term used in reference to a cat's fur. The major qualifiers in this regard are long and shorthaired.

Crate – Any small container that can be securely locked and that is used to temporarily confine a cat or other companion animal for the purposes of safe transport is referred to as a "crate".

Crepuscular – Animals that exhibit crepuscular behavior are most active at dawn and dusk, which is the accurate term for the most active periods in a cat's day. It is not correct to say that these animals are nocturnal, even though they do possess excellent low light vision.

Crossbred – Any cat that is the product of a mating between a dam and a sire of different breeds is crossbred. This may occur as an accident or as an intentional effort to create a new and distinct breed exhibiting desirable qualities of the two foundation breeds.

D

Dam – In a mating pair of cats, the female is often referred to as the "dam".

Dander – Dander refers to the small scales that are shed along with the hair of an animal that are often created by saliva that dried on the fur as a consequence of self-grooming. Dander plays a leading role in the triggering of allergic reactions in people with specific sensitivity. In cats, the presence of the protein Fel d 1 in the dander is mainly responsible for this reaction in humans.

Declawing – Declawing is an extremely controversial surgical procedure in which the last digit of the cat's toes are removed so that the animal is permanently deprived of its claws. In theory the procedure developed as an anti-scratching measure, but it is now seen as excessive and cruel and is illegal in Europe and many parts of the United States.

Desex – "Desexing" is an accepted term to describe the procedures, either spaying or neutering, whereby animals are deprived of their ability to reproduce.

Domesticated – Domesticated animals are those creatures that, through long association, have come to be tame and to live in companionship with humans either to work or to serve as companions.

E

Ear Mites – Ear mites are microscopic parasites often present in the ear canals of felines. They cause redness and irritation, leading to an accumulation of black, tarry debris and often secondary yeast infections. This is an extremely unpleasant infestation for the cat accompanied by extreme itching. It is detectable not only by the visible inflammation, but also by the presence of a strong and unpleasant odor.

Entire – Entire is a term used in the cat fancy to describe an animal that has not been spayed or neutered and therefore has an intact reproductive system.

Exhibitor – An exhibitor is an individual who participates in a cat show either with a cat he or she owns or as a representative of the owner.

F

Fel d 1 – The protein Fel d 1 can be found in the sebaceous glands and saliva of cats. It is responsible for causing an allergic reaction in humans who have a specific sensitivity to it. This reaction includes, but is not limited so, sneezing, watering eyes, nasal congestion and itching.

Feline - A feline is any animal that is a member of the family Felidae. This group includes "big" cats like lions, tigers, and jaguars, as well as domestic cats.

Fleas – Fleas are parasites of the order Siphonaptera that feed on the blood of the host animal they infest. These creatures do not have wings, but are well adapted to jump.

Flehmening/Flehmen Reaction – In cats, the Flehmen Reaction is often mistaken as a facial grimace indicating dislike. In reality, this "expression" during which the cat holds its mouth partially open is adopted for the express purpose of allowing air to pass over a special structure in the roof of the mouth just behind the upper front teeth called Jacobsen's Organ. The organ, which is two small holes, functions as a secondary set of nostrils giving the cat the ability to essentially "taste" a scent or odor.

G

Gene pool – The gene pool in any population of organisms refers to the collective genetic information of the group relative to its diversity and reproduction.

Genes – Genes are the distinct hereditary units responsible for specific characteristics passed down from one generation of organisms to another. Genes consist of a DNA sequence found at a specific location on a chromosome.

Genetic – The term genetics is used in reference to any inherited trait or characteristic identifiable from one generation to the next.

Genetically Linked Defects – Any specific health or physical problem passed from one generation to the next that is, in some way, negative, harmful, or potentially limiting in nature.

Genetics – Genetics is the scientific study of heredity.

Genotype – A genotype is the term referring to the genetic makeup of an organism or a group of organisms.

Groom – Grooming refers to the procedures and protocols involved in caring for the coat of a cat including, but not limited to brushing, combing, trimming or washing.

Guard Hair – Guard hairs are longer, coarser hairs that form the outer or top layer of the coat on some breeds of cat.

H

Heat – "Heat" is the commonly accepted term to designate when a female cat reaches the point in seasonal estrus when she is ready to be impregnated by a male.

Hereditary – Hereditary elements including traits, diseases, or conditions are genetically transmitted from parents to their offspring.

Histamine - Histamines are physiologically active amines present in plant and animal tissue that are released from musk cells as part of an allergic reaction.

Hock – In anatomical nomenclature, a hock is that part of a cat's hind leg we would describe as the animal's "ankle".

Housetraining – Housetraining or housebreaking is the process of training a cat to live cleanly in a home with humans utilizing a litter box or pan.

Humane Societies – Humane societies are, in a general sense, groups working to end animal suffering as a consequence of overt cruelty, impoverishment or similar circumstances. The umbrella organization in the United States is The Humane Society of the United States and in the United Kingdom it is Humane Society International.

I

Immunization – Immunization is the targeted use of injections for the purpose of cultivating immunity against disease. The injections are also commonly called vaccinations.

Innate – When a quality, tendency or trait is said to be innate, it has been present since birth.

Inbreeding – The act of inbreeding occurs when two cats with a close filial relationship, like siblings, mate and produce offspring. Typically this results in genetic flaws that become more serious the deeper the inbreeding penetrates into the gene pool.

Instinct – Instincts are patterns of behavior that are innate and come in automatic response to triggering stimuli in the environment.

Intact - Animals with complete reproductive systems are said to be intact because they are still capable of producing offspring.

J

Jacobsen's Organ – In cats the Jacobsen's Organ is found just behind the upper front teeth on the roof of the mouth. It is comprised of two small openings that function as second nostrils that allow the cat to "taste" odors or scents.

K

Kindle – Kindle is a collective term that refers to a group of cats in one place at one time. Another word with the same meaning is "chowder".

Kitten – A cat is said to be a kitten when it is less than six months of age.

L

Lactation – Lactation is the physical process by which mammary glands produce and secrete milk for the nourishment of young mammals.

Litter – Litter is the collective term for all kittens born at one time to a single mother. Typically this is 3-4, but some litters can be as large as 6-10 or even 12-14 in some breeds.

Litter Box – Litter boxes are really any container of any configuration that is used for the express purpose of providing an indoor cat with a sanitary location to urinate and defecate in a provided collecting material like clay gravel or fine clumping sand.

Longhair – Longhair is a descriptive term for the coat of a cat that is marked by flowing length of fur, plumed tails and neck ruffs.

M

Mites - Small arachnids (*Acarina*) are parasites that infest both animals and plants and are often found in the ear canals of felines.

Moggy – Moggy is a term in the United Kingdom for a mixed breed cat.

Muzzle – A cat's muzzle is that part of the head that projects forward and includes the mouth, jaws and nose. It may alternately be referred to as the snout.

N

Neuter – Neuter is a term that specifically refers to the castration of a male cat to prevent the animal from impregnating females.

Nictitating Membrane – The nictating membrane, or third eyelid, on a cat is an inner transparent eyelid that works to moisten and protect the eye.

Nocturnal – Animals that are nocturnal are most active during the night. This term is mistakenly applied to cats. Felines are actually crepuscular, meaning they are most active at dawn and dusk.

O

Odd-Eyed – When a cat is "odd-eyed" it has two eyes of different colors.

P

Papers – A cat's "papers" are the official documentation of the animal's registered pedigree verifying the authenticity of its lineage as part of a designated breed.

Pedigree - A pedigree is essentially a cat's family tree or genealogy set in writing and covering three or more generations. The record is used to clearly establish the animal's genetic authenticity within a specific breed.

Pet Quality – Purebred cats that are designated to be "pet quality" have some physical characteristic or characteristics that diverge sufficiently from the accepted standard for the breed that they are not considered candidates to be shown or to be used in a breeding program.

Q

Queen – A female cat with an intact reproductive system is called a queen.

Quick – The quick of a cat's claw is the vascular "pink" just behind the white nail that will bleed profusely if it is accidentally clipped.

R

Rabies – Rabies is a highly infectious viral disease typically fatal to warm-blooded animals. It is transmitted by a bite from an infected individual and attacks the central nervous system causing severely aggressive behavior.

Registered Name - The registered name of a cat is the official name used by the registering agency on the animal's pedigree. The name is typically long and contains multiple references to the ancestry of the individual.

S

Scratching Post - A scratching "post" is any structure covered in carpet, rope, or similar material that has been constructed for the express purpose of allowing a domestic cat to sharpen and clean its claws without being destructive to household furnishings.

Shelter – A shelter is any local or regional organization that works to rescue and care for stray, homeless animals with the end goal of placing them in permanent homes.

Show Quality – Show quality cats are individuals that meet the official breed standard for their type and are thus recognized as suitable to be exhibited in cat shows and to be used in breeding programs.

Sire – In a breeding pair of cats, the sire is the male member.

Spay – Spaying is the procedure whereby the ovaries of a female cat are removed to render the animal incapable of producing offspring.

Spray – Spraying is territorial behavior most typically present in male cats involving the emissions of a stream of pungent urine to serve as a territorial marker.

Stud – Studs are male cats that have intact testicles so that they are suitable to serve as half of a mating pair in a breeding program.

T

Tapetum Lucidum - The tapetum lucidum is the interior portion of the feline eye that is highly reflective and aids in night vision. This is the portion of the eye that glows in photographs taken with a flash.

V

Vaccine - A vaccine is a preparation of a weakened or dead pathogen like a bacterium or virus. The vaccine is used to stimulate antibody production for the purpose of creating immunity against disease.

W

Wean – Weaning is the point at which a mother cat breaks her kittens away from subsisting on the milk she produces so that they begin to draw their primary nutrition from solid food.

Whisker Pad - The whisker pad is the thickened area on either side of a cat's face where the animal's sensory whiskers are anchored.

Whole – A whole cat is an individual of either gender with a functioning reproductive system.

References

The Complete Cat Breed Book. DK. April 2013.

Helgren, J. Anne. *Encyclopedia of Cat Breeds*. Barron's Educational Series, April 2013.

Richards, James. *ASPCA Complete Guide to Cats: Everything You Need to Know About Choosing and Caring for Your Pet*. Chronicle Books. September, 1999.

Rixon, Angela. *The Illustrated Encyclopedia of Cat Breeds*. Wellfleet Press, January 2011.

Boroff, Paula, "Birmans: The Sacred Cats of Burma," The Cat Fanciers' Asociation, (Accessed April 2014), www.cfainc.org/Breeds/BreedsAB/Birman/BirmanArticle.aspx

Cummings, Karen. Guide to Owning a Birman Cat. Popular Cat Library, 1999.

IAMS Guide to Cat Breeds: Birman, (Accessed April 2014), www.iams.com/pet-health/cat-breeds/birman

Maggitti, Phil and Michelle Earle-Bridges. Birman Cats (Barron's Complete Pet Owner's Manuals). Barron's Educational Series, 1996.

All Photographs : www.bigstockphoto.com

Cover Design:- Liliana Gonzalez Garcia, ipublicidades.com
(info@ipublicidades.com)

Index

E

F

G

H

L

T

U

V

W

CPSIA information can be obtained
at www.ICGtesting.com
Printed in the USA
BVOW11s0404070717
488550BV00006B/156/P